"A wonderful read! It applies lessons fr(
marketing to illustrate seven ways to imp
business—all with Jeff's entertaining and instructive
gift of storytelling."

**David Aaker, Consultant; Professor Emeritus, University of California,
Berkeley, Haas School of Business; Vice Chairman, Prophet; Author of 15
books, including *Creating Signature Stories***

"Jeff has actually set up the marketing equation. Each principle
he cites has its own immense value but when the seven are
combined, they perform exponentially."

Niraj Dawar, Professor, Marketing, Ivey Business School

"Beyond all the data, big and small, beyond all the research
methods, beyond all the theory, the essential truth is that marketing
is about making an emotional connection with your audience. In
his book, Jeff brilliantly demonstrates how successful marketing
connects people with products and people with people."

Bob Scarpelli, Former Chairman and Chief Creative Officer, DDB Worldwide

"In an intimate narrative style, Jeff delivers a succinct reflection of
the history of marketing and identifies the seven principles that
guide it. In doing so, he tells the story (one of his own principles!)
of how the tenets remain, despite constantly changing context.
So, while consumer expectations may evolve, these principles do
not. Jeff expertly weaves the past with the present and the science
with the art for an entertaining and educative read."

Mary Chambers, Chief Strategy Officer, McCann Worldgroup Canada

"Jeff has done the improbable. Not only has he developed a
simple framework that business builders need to employ to
establish enduring customer relationships, he's also written a page-
turner of a book. I read it in a single, compelling sitting."

Howard Belk, Co-CEO, Chief Creative Officer, Siegel+Gale

"Marketing is about some of these things some of the time and all of these things all of the time. You cannot address community without experience and authenticity without story. Overall, the seven principles framed are the abiding and enduring points of marketing."

Mark Tungate, Author of *Media Monoliths: How Media Brands Thrive and Survive; Adland: A Global History of Advertising;* and *Branded Beauty: How Marketing Changed the Way We Look*

"Distilled from his decades of branding, media and marketing experience, Jeff presents a set of highly relevant and critical principles for today's ultra-competitive and global business landscape. A great read. Enjoy!"

Chris Stefanyk, Head of Brand Partnerships, Wattpad

"Jeff boldly states, 'no brand is for everyone.' Marketing, when done right, connects with the most desired consumer and makes that connection real. It takes a smart marketer to know they cannot appeal to all and it takes a savvy marketer to use the seven principles in this book. It is filled with timeless examples that bring each principle to life with entertaining storytelling that makes them stick."

Jani Yates, President and CEO, Ad Standards

"At a time when the role of marketing is being both elevated yet hyper-scrutinized in large organizations, Jeff does an outstanding job extracting the essence of marketing in seven core principles. This is a great tool for marketers, but an even greater asset for those organizations who appreciate but may be a bit incredulous of the true value of marketing in today's changing world."

Wes B. Wilkes, VP, Head of Global Brand Strategy, MetLife

"For a great many businesses, "marketing digitally" is a solution or a campaign idea all on its own. They confuse tactics with strategy. Jeff smartly reminds us all that while marketing channels have evolved over the last century, the fundamentals of marketing have not. Get inspired, read on."

James Connell, Vice President, E-Commerce & Customer Experience, Roots

"In today's digital, fast-paced environment, the powerful emotional connection to a brand's narrative remains to drives loyalty. In his book, Jeff takes a pragmatic look at how seven fundamental principles contribute to the building of that narrative and combine to drive brand growth."

Pino Di Ioia, CEO, Beavertails

"This book provides seven principles that marketers cannot ignore. Second, it brings them to life with cases from marketing's history that engage and illuminate. Lastly, it doesn't read like a traditional business book which is a good thing. Jeff has packaged compelling content in an entertaining narrative and it absolutely works."

Bob Macdonald, CEO, Bond Brand Loyalty

"In this age of unlimited choices, the need to create demand is more important than ever. This new book lays out the enduring principles of marketing that have been relevant for decades and remain relevant today. Jeff lucidly explains each principle using entertaining case studies to engage the reader and to stimulate reflection, thought and action."

Lulu Raghavan, Managing Director, Landor

"Jeff references a quote from Arianna Huffington that 'marketers need to be master storytellers.' I'm still trying to decide whether Jeff is more of a storyteller who loves marketing or a marketer who loves storytelling. Either way, this is an entertaining read that energizes the basic principles of good marketing with stories from the past and present that are as fun to read as they are enlightening to marketing practitioners."

Gordon McMillan, CEO and Chief Creative Officer, McMillan

"Jeff points out in his brand-building principles the marketing equation is not new. What is new is now more than ever we need to pay close attention to the evolution and marketing in the year in which we live. The camera is now the pen in storytelling. The mobile phone is the main viewing screen. Facebook, YouTube and Snapchat are what were once ABC, CBS, and NBC. The principles in his book are the guardrails and goalposts for marketing in our era and eras to come."

James Orsini, Chief Operating Officer, Vayner Media

"I'm lucky to have worked with Jeff on some great projects. His insights always have huge value. So does his incredible book that proves successful marketing results from telling truthful, emotional, and compelling stories. Jeff provides the way to create and market your brand."

Ash Modha, CEO, Mondetta Clothing Co.

"Jeff shares fascinating stories of marketing successes and failures to develop a core set of brand-building principles. Written with the ease of a master storyteller, Jeff provides a colourful and insightful look at marketing, grounded in experience and verified by research. A much needed, fresh look."

Rick Nason, Partner, RSD Solutions; Associate Professor of Finance, Dalhousie University; Author of *It's Not Complicated: The Art and Science of Complexity in Business*

WHY
MARKETING
WORKS

7 TIME-TESTED, BRAND-BUILDING PRINCIPLES

WHY
MARKETING
WORKS

7 TIME-TESTED, BRAND-BUILDING PRINCIPLES

JEFF SWYSTUN

BRIGANTINE MEDIA

Why Marketing Works
7 Time-Tested, Brand-Building Principles

Copyright © 2019 by Jeff Swystun

Published by Brigantine Media
211 North Ave., St. Johnsbury, Vermont 05819

ISBN 978-1-9384067-5-1

For more information on this book, please contact:
Brigantine Media
211 North Avenue, St. Johnsbury, Vermont 05819
Phone: 802-751-8802
Email: neil@brigantinemedia.com
Website: www.brigantinemedia.com

Dedication

This book was made possible because of the marketers I have learned from and laughed with (a group too numerous to list). Thanks to my teachers and professors, my talented colleagues at extremely impressive organizations, and my clients who share risk and reward as we jointly solve complex business problems through branding and marketing.

I owe intellectual curiosity to my mother.
From my father, I gained a benchmark of trust and integrity.
Together, they taught me to laugh, be generous, entertain, and celebrate whatever life delivers.
My wife, Lois, stuck with me through every phase of this book. She deserves co-authorship.

CONTENTS

INTRODUCTION

It was a beautiful summer day. Not one to be wasted. A slight breeze and warming sun suggested many different activities. Perhaps a round of golf or boating to a secluded spot or a hike on a trail not yet explored. But none of these were to be. Instead, I found myself holding two reusable shopping bags as I lagged behind my wife, cursing my misfortune.

She insisted we visit the local farmers market. In the interests of sustained marital bliss, I joined a stream of people heading in the same direction. Entering the market, we were greeted by lively banter between vendors and customers. On a transformed civic parking lot were rows of tented stalls and displays, a rich assortment of the staples people require and luxuries they desire.

One seller enthusiastically showcased generous cuts of meat. Beef, pork, rabbit, goose, quail, and venison were artfully staged. I was drawn to a booth from a local restaurant. The chef gave a cooking demonstration using local ingredients. Smart, I thought. Cool marketing.

"Summer salads demand freshness," he declared. "Fresh ingredients and fresh ideas. Today we will make a roasted beet salad with crumbled blue cheese and a tantalizing array of nuts. On top, I add lime and thinly sliced avocado." People were taking notes and snapping pictures. "Next we will make parmesan pepper curly kale chips." *What is with this kale craze?*

Craving caffeine, I ordered two coffees at a very un-Starbucks stand. The barista and I exchanged pleasantries while he soft-sold me on a bag of beans. I ended up buying two. My wife and I sipped our steaming cups and sauntered over to the produce stands. Corn, cucumbers, cauliflower, and broccoli showed off rich colors and earthy fragrances.

Most shoppers were not filling a prepared list. They were improvising and basing meals on what they happened upon. In neighboring stalls were plums, apricots, strawberries, blackberries, and blueberries. These were so appealing that they almost sold themselves. But promotion was evident. The vendors were adept at drawing people in with samples and conversation. Selling was underway, but it was authentic and entertaining.

A warm, pleasant smell caught my attention. I spied potato rosemary bread next to zucchini mushroom buns. My wife selected a kale loaf and I rolled my eyes. *Kale again?*

Displayed near the breads were cakes, cookies, pastries, muffins, croissants, pies, tarts, and flans. Friendly rivalries among the vendors could be seen, as hummus was positioned against chutneys and guacamoles battled salsas. These dips, sauces, and marinades gave way to oils derived from olives, corn, sunflower, peanuts, and palm. Jams, preserves, marmalades, and cheeses were well stocked and stacked.

I was enjoying myself and admitted this to my wife. Even better, I started thinking about this book.

The farmers market in the Old Village of Mont Tremblant, Quebec—its promotions, product explanations, negotiations, and transactions—got me mulling over the words "market" and "marketing." "Market" refers to a group of sellers and buyers who cooperate to exchange goods and services in a public gathering. "Marketing" has roots in Latin, as so many words do, and is comprised of *merx* or "merchandise" and *mercari* or "to trade." The words reference the acts of buying and selling.

Marketplaces are similar from continent to continent, country to country, and town to town. And people have been selling and buying in markets all around the world for centuries. Products to satisfy our needs and our wants have been on display from the ancient open-air markets to today's websites—from Pompeii to eBay. And yes, this includes kale.

You may not know that marketing, just like markets, has existed since mankind's earliest time. It has been there to help sell products and services using every kind of communication from hieroglyphics to the town crier to radio, television, and Facebook. When you look, you'll find an amazing consistency, sophistication, and continuity in the practice of marketing throughout history.

I've examined marketing throughout the ages to the present day and have boiled it down to the seven reasons why marketing works:

1   Marketing offers **solutions** to problems.

2   Marketing tells **stories**, which people naturally respond to.

3   Marketing that leverages **emotion** compels.

4   Marketing builds **relationships** between customers and products.

5   Marketing creates **community**.

6   Marketing delivers **experiences**.

7   Marketing demands **authenticity** to be fully believed, especially today.

I think you'll be surprised to find how much similarity there is at the core of marketing throughout the ages. Still, there is much to be learned from marketing campaigns both past and present. It is clear that through the centuries marketing has worked.

Marketing works best when it simultaneously employs these seven time-tested principles. Think of these as a checklist for your marketing. Each element has to be in place and work in concert with each other. Throughout history, the most successful companies and brands have consistently used these principles to stand out and to sell more, efficiently and effectively. So, let's go on a fun and informative marketing journey.

CHAPTER 1

MARKETING OFFERS SOLUTIONS

"Making the solution seem so completely inevitable and obvious,
so uncontrived and natural - it's so hard!"[1]

SIR JONATHAN PAUL IVE, CHIEF DESIGN OFFICER, APPLE INC.

Imagine that you and I have a time machine. Let's set the controls for 1898 because I have something important to show you. Our destination is the headquarters of the National Biscuit Company in East Hanover, New Jersey.

We arrive back in time to witness a man addressing a large group of employees. He speaks with a strong voice full of passion and conviction. The man tells the assembly to "bear yourselves as men of decency, of honesty, of character," and "do nothing to disgrace or discredit that emblem that you carry with you."[2] The audience is visibly moved. The "emblem" that employees are told never to disgrace is the company's logo. The words and sentiment are a rallying cry.

The speaker is the company's leader, Adolphus Green, a Harvard graduate who began his career as a corporate lawyer. His job as legal advisor to different enterprises provided the inspiration to form the American Biscuit and Manufacturing Company in 1890. Eight years and forty acquisitions later it became the National Biscuit Company. Eventually, the National Biscuit Company would be known as Nabisco (now a subsidiary of Mondelēz International) and today it sells more than 320 million pounds of snack foods annually.

Green demonstrated the scrappiness and tenacity of someone born the eleventh of eleven children. He inherited his formidable work ethic from his mother, whose boarding house supported the family following the untimely death of his father. Green's leadership was driven by a fervent belief in the solutions Nabisco innovated for customers. He built a military-religious culture within the business. In fact, business was Green's purpose and love. "I have been told that there is no poetry or romance in business," said Green, "but since I left the practice of the law to undertake this work, I have found enough inspiration in it to rival that which moved the crusaders of old."[3]

The National Biscuit Company's first nationally launched product had Green's imprint all over it. The product had a playful name: Uneeda Biscuit. The lawyer-turned-marketer influenced every aspect of the brand from name to logo to packaging to advertising. He even wrote marketing copy: "Uneeda Biscuit. Served with every meal; take a box with you on your travels; splendid for sandwiches; perfect for picnics; unequalled for general use; does not contain sugar. This is a perfect food for everybody, and the prices place them within the reach of all."

Those words do not roll smoothly off the tongue but you have to appreciate the list of extensive benefits Green chose to highlight. He viewed Uneeda Biscuits as more than a new product. They were a unique solution for the family pantry and Green wanted every single consumer to experience the difference. Always ambitious, he saw the entirety of America as his market.

In a decision pivotal to Uneeda Biscuits' success, Green hired N.W. Ayer, the first advertising agency formed in the United States, to make Uneeda Biscuits a household name. N.W. Ayer was one of the most influential advertising agencies of all time. Founded in Philadelphia in 1869, the agency cemented brands into people's consciousness by positioning products as solutions.

The agency was an innovator early on. *Advertising Age* credits N.W. Ayer as having "pioneered the use of fine art in advertising and established the industry's first art department. It was the first agency to use a full-time copywriter and the first to institute a copy department."[4] N.W. Ayer was also the first agency to advertise on the radio airwaves.[5]

N.W. Ayer did more than create marketing and advertising campaigns—it influenced business strategies. At the turn of the twentieth century, the piano maker Steinway & Sons was selling only to the wealthy and to concert halls. N.W. Ayer recommended to the company that it add a range of more affordable pianos. The accompanying marketing campaign hinted at social cachet for those who purchased a piano and sophistication for those who learned to play. Steinway pianos became a fixture in hundreds of thousands of homes worldwide. N.W. Ayer created a vast new market for Steinway.

By linking business strategy and marketing, N.W. Ayer articulated a brand's purpose and the solution it provided. The agency created the "When it rains it pours" tagline and now-famous Morton Salt girl to tell consumers that the salt was premium quality and would always flow. The agency penned the slogan "I'd walk a mile for a Camel" for R. J. Reynolds Tobacco in 1921, speaking to the convenience and quality of an already-rolled cigarette. N.W. Ayer leveraged emotion with the "Reach out and touch someone" campaign for AT&T that prompted millions to phone loved ones more often. It summed up pride, service and self-accomplishment with the slogan "Be all that you can be" for the United States Army.

N.W. Ayer's marketing tugged at heartstrings, produced smiles, and promised consumers something more, something better. It advertised solutions for the problems of people's daily lives. This approach was evident in the work for Uneeda Biscuit.

The 1899 Uneeda Biscuit campaign holds the distinction for being the world's first to cost over one million dollars. N.W. Ayer designed it to dribble out a little information at a time to create interest. This is now known as a "teaser" campaign, whose purpose is to get people interested and talking. It draws one in with speculation of what is to come.

The campaign began when one word appeared in magazines, newspapers, and on billboards across America: "Uneeda." Tongues were soon wagging about what it could be. The next round of advertisements told consumers, "Uneeda Biscuit." Now people knew the product but didn't know what made it special. Next, the campaign asked, "Do you know Uneeda Biscuit?"

The series ended with a confident and playful conclusion: "Of course Uneeda Biscuit." The verbal creativity and the reach of the campaign succeeded in getting the brand on people's lips and the product into their mouths.

Adolphus Green was comfortable with the audacious campaign because he had faith in the quality of the product and the inventiveness of the packaging. In 1899, people shopped in bulk from neighborhood stores. Consumers were all too familiar with the dirty cracker barrel. Broken, soggy, and infested crackers were the norm. Green was on a mission to render the cracker barrel obsolete.

Nabisco had discovered a solution to protect the biscuits from deterioration due to moisture, contamination, and breakage. Uneeda Biscuit came in a new moisture-protected package that sheltered the biscuit and maintained freshness longer. Today we are familiar with this packaging of crackers and cereals, but when it first came out, it was a modern miracle. Shoppers picked a pristine package from the shelf rather than have a clerk root around in a contaminated barrel.

This packaging allowed the company to bake a lighter, flakier, and more appealing cracker. The new package, by lengthening the cracker's shelf life, made national distribution possible.[6] Green was spending unprecedented money by selling Uneeda Biscuits nationwide and needed smart marketing to convince consumers that this change was beneficial.

Part of the advertising budget went to an army of sign painters. The Uneeda Biscuit brand appeared on the exterior walls of buildings across the country. (Today there are forums on Flickr, the photo-sharing site, profiling these beautiful but fading pieces of marketing history. From time to time, a building will be torn down to reveal another classic hand-painted advertisement on a neighboring wall.)

The campaign was a success. Within its first year, an astonishing ten million packages were sold every month, more than twenty times the combined sales of all other packaged crackers! The Uneeda Biscuit campaign became a template for Nabisco. Every new product was positioned as a solution. Animal Crackers were both food and playthings. They allowed children to eat a bear, crocodile, giraffe, and zebra as part of their school lunches. Nabisco still sells over forty million boxes annually, according to the company's website. (I wonder if McDonald's took inspiration from Nabisco for their Happy Meals.) The company also brought out other cookies: Lorna Doone, Mallomar, and Oreo.

The popularity of the Oreo is undeniable but few know that it was not original. The first treat to consist of two chocolate disks with a sweet cream filling came from the Sunshine Company. It was called the Hydrox cookie. The Hydrox may have been hurt by its name, given that it sounds like a corrosive cleaning product. As the Oreo took off, Hydrox suffered from the perception of being a less dynamic imitation. In its first one hundred years of production, over 450 billion Oreo cookies were devoured worldwide. In 2015, $2.9 billion worth of the treats were sold.[7] It is the best selling cookie in the world.

In 2009, Nabisco discontinued the Uneeda biscuit. After 110 years sales had slid, and (pun intended) the product had grown stale. But the biscuit outlasted N.W. Ayer. The parent company of N.W. Ayer, Publicis, closed the agency down in 2002.

IT'S NOT THE MATTRESS

There is an adage in the marketing industry that says, "Don't sell the mattress, sell the sleep." This cleverly and concisely captures the idea of marketing a solution. In this case, it speaks to the benefits one receives from a quality mattress. To further explore this time-tested principle of marketing, I sat down with Chris Hummel, Chief Marketing Officer of United Rentals. The largest equipment rental company in the world, United Rentals has over 880 locations throughout the United States and Canada and $1.5 billion in annual revenue.

"Successful companies present solutions that make people's lives easier and more enjoyable. When marketers talk about selling solutions, what they are trying to do is make the product indispensible. They communicate so that people see how the product fits and how it can improve their lives," said Chris. He pointed to companies like Netflix and Apple, who position their products as solutions for everyday life or to enhance that life.

This principle applies to businesses of any size, from United Rentals to the neighborhood drycleaner. Chris has witnessed the marketing of solutions at the companies where he has worked. "There is a tipping point where you become customer-centric— where the customer's needs start to guide the business. You ask: 'What role does my product or service play in people lives?' and 'How do I market so it solves a customer's need or want?' You engage in a conversation and have to understand your customers intimately. Customers stop being a faceless mass and become your brother, your friend, your neighbor."

A SHAVE SO SMOOTH

Solutions are highly personal even though the same solution may be used by millions of people. Take the Gillette razor. Around the time people discovered they needed a certain biscuit, another businessman was solving the problem of the daily shave. King Camp Gillette was an innovator and intuitive marketer. His legacy is a thin, inexpensive, and disposable blade of steel.

Gillette got his start at the Crown Cork and Seal Company that held the patent for the cap on carbonated beverages. While selling for Crown Cork, he witnessed a practice that sparked his own invention. Consumers threw away the bottle caps once opened. A product that was used once and then discarded fascinated Gillette. One morning while shaving he thought the same concept could work for razors. With disposable blades, people would no longer need to sharpen expensive blades, which was difficult for many people to do well, and they could spend less time on the whole shaving process. Consumers would get a faster, simpler, and closer shave.

Gillette's disposable razor was not an instant success. Sales for 1903 were 51 razors and 168 blades.[8] So he turned his attention to marketing. Gillette popularized its razor and disposable blades through a series of creative campaigns.

One advertisement became a pop culture favorite, although it looks very weird now. It features a cherubic smiling infant clutching a silver Gillette razor in a chubby hand. Shaving soap is slopped on one cheek. The copy reads, "Gillette Safety Razor" coupled with the slogan, "Begin Early. Shave Yourself."

Today the advertisement is criticized because it features a baby in the sale of a dangerous product, but at the time the infant helped communicate a critical benefit. The connection to "smooth as a baby's bottom" was easily inferred. Another ad asked, "What excuse can a man give nowadays for appearing with an unshaved face?" That ad asked men whether they were meeting society's standards for appearance.

The notions of simplicity and ease of use resonated. The following year, sales grew to 90,884 razors and 123,648 blades.[9] Gillette's invention has inspired product developers and marketers ever since. Selling two items to make one solution such as a razor and the blade is also seen in products such as inkjet printers that need cartridges, Swiffers that require special cloths, and Nespresso machines that brew with coffee pods.

By 1915, razor sales reached 450,000 units and blade sales hit an astounding 70 million.[10] The business kept growing by stressing it was a time saver, a tool to ensure success, and a more hygienic option. Gillette's razor and disposable blades became a problem-solver. This contextual focus on solutions satisfies marketing guru Peter Drucker's view that, "The purpose of business is to create and keep a customer." You do that by offering a solution.

A WHEELY GOOD IDEA

When Steve Jobs was asked how much consumer research played a role in the launch of the iPad, he replied, "None. It isn't the consumers' job to know what they want."[11] Jobs was expressing his belief that consumers cannot always identify or articulate their needs and wants.

Before Apple came along, Sony was the innovator in personal technologies with the Walkman, mini-TVs, videocassette recorders, and the Discman. Sony co-founder Akio Morita, who oversaw these new products, subscribed to the same view as Jobs. In a presentation to the media he stated, "Our plan is to lead the public with new products rather than ask them what kind of products they want. The public does not know what is possible, but we do."[12]

The most effective and enduring brands are often born from a single insight into how we behave. This insight can be so simple that people react by saying, "Why didn't I think of that?" or "That must already exist." Take wheeled luggage, for example. It took us a long time to come up with the idea but now we cannot imagine living without it.

In 1972, Bernard Sadow tugged an odd-looking prototype of a rolling suitcase into Macy's. He had to do this several times to convince the luggage buyer (showing that persistence is often critical to success). Sadow's inspiration had come one day in 1970 when he was lugging two large suitcases through an airport and a man breezed by towing heavy machinery on a dolly.[13] This led him to the idea of luggage that coasted on small wheels and could be pulled by a leash. The first prototypes were poorly balanced and tended to topple over, but they were a huge improvement over carrying a hefty load.

Seventeen years after Sadow's inspiration, Northwest Airlines pilot Robert Plath developed the Rollaboard suitcase for flight crews. His design resembles what we enjoy today. I spend a great deal of time traveling and continue to marvel at this simple idea that has had such impact. To me, the word "luggage" means to lug, to be uncomfortable, to be a human beast of burden. It took a long time and two keen observers to shatter that notion. The best insights produce solutions that, once introduced, feel like they have always been there.

Recently I spoke at a design conference in Shenzhen, China. A fellow speaker was Paul Gardien, Vice President of Philips Design. Philips is a solutions machine. Every day it is obsessing over products and services in electronics, healthcare, and lighting. The company is the largest global supplier of lighting.

Paul shared what Philips is doing to provide cool solutions in healthcare—specifically, how children interact with CT machines and the scanning process. Undergoing a test at the hospital is stressful for anyone, but Paul asked the audience to imagine what that experience would be like for a child. "It's a scary environment for them. So what we did was make a small scanner replica that the hospital staff uses to educate the kids on what will happen and what the process will be."

Philips uses experience flows or customer relationship journeys to understand needs and wants. According to Paul, "We don't look at an MRI scanner or an ultrasound as a single product. We look at the complete journey throughout the hospital. Design is more and more about the total experience, an immersive solution. This links closely with marketing by asking, 'How do you encounter a product? How do you choose a product? How do you 'unpack' the experience to make it clear and easy for people?" In other words, how do you make it a *solution*?

Philips Design proposed a new system to support children, their parents, and the technician during the process from preparation to completion of the exam. Children are now introduced to a room with soothing colors, plush furniture, and fun motifs. Interactive kiosks educate the children on what they will experience.

The centerpiece of this effort is the Kitten Scanner, a toy CT machine. An article about it in *The International Journal of Design* was written by Paul and his colleagues. "By choosing a toy and placing it into the scanner, a child triggers an animated story that helps the child understand the procedure in an entertaining way. The child can see that if the toy is shaken in the scanner, the image distorts, so they understand that they must lie still to get a good image. The type of toy that a child chooses then affects the personalization of the examination room through animated projections and lighting. The technician can use these effects to guide a child comfortably through the procedure."

Children now go faster and more accurately through the scanners. They are made as comfortable as possible. Philips Design found that a child is more likely to be compliant when provided with a simple explanation of what will happen and why. Paul believes the process is all about personalizing a solution. "It is simple. We need to treat people the way we want to be treated."

The sales of Philips MRI machines has risen versus competitors. The company worked with hospitals and clinics to provide a holistic solution that has made the job easier for medical professionals and put children at ease.

THE CADILLAC OF THIS
AND THE UBER OF THAT

The Cadillac automobile has been a symbol of prestige since its launch in 1902. Over time, the phrase, "The Cadillac of such-and-such," has been used as high praise when marketing other products. Hillquist, a machinery manufacturer in Denver, sold "the Cadillac of all trim saws" and Rock-Ola was "the Cadillac of phonographs." General Motors never objected to these comparisons because they raised the status of the car. It helped make Cadillac synonymous with quality. Being the 'Cadillac of something' was shorthand for being better than the rest.[14]

There is a new phrase these days. Companies are now being called "the Uber of ___." Wag is called the Uber of dog walking, Saucey is the Uber of liquor, GreenPal is the Uber of lawn care. Cadillac was considered the pinnacle of quality; Uber is now synonymous with business model reinvention.

Uber's car service has upended the transportation industry and attracted controversy and advocates at the same time. Despite protests against Uber from cab companies and challenges from governments around the world, people continue to download the Uber app to arrange rides with Uber drivers. As of late 2018, the Uber website shows that service is available in over 84 countries and 858 cities, and the business may be valued at $120 billion at its initial public offering in 2019, after just ten years of existence.[15]

This has prompted countless companies to copy Uber's business model, now referred to in the startup world as "Uberification."[16] It defines being disruptive to the status quo. Uber presents a solution on multiple levels. It gives consumers a transportation choice beyond taxis, buses, or subways. The experience puts control literally in the hands of the customer. You track the car that is picking you up by following it on your smartphone, so the timing is transparent. No cash exchanges hands, because the passenger's credit card is charged and a receipt is sent by email.

The Uber-way is part of "the sharing economy" or what is called "collaborative consumption." Participants have access to shared products or services. Uber smartly uses up excess inventory and makes the world a more efficient place. Cars already manufactured are employed to move people from place to place. People looking for supplemental income can become drivers. In larger cities, it has allowed some residents to avoid purchasing a car.

Uber has extended its model. UberEATS allows consumers to choose food with the tap of a smartphone and have those selections delivered quickly. UberEATS offers a handpicked lineup of restaurants and makes sure the restaurants' menu options are delivery-friendly. UberEATS curates restaurants in each city where it operates. Instead of simply acting as a delivery service, UberEATS provides value to restaurant partners through exclusivity and marketing. The company involves restaurants in the entire process, including brainstorming on how to better reach consumers.[17]

UberEATS has rolled out slowly, allowing the company to monitor feedback and react in real time to that feedback. Initially, customers complained about the lack of vegetarian selections. That was quickly corrected. In fact, the lineup of food options is constantly being adjusted based on consumer feedback.

The top dishes ordered through UberEATS in Manhattan show how varied and exotic the selections can be. Residents order up Mighty Quinn's brisket sandwich, INDAY's "Not Rice" bowl, Veselka's handmade pierogi big plate, Ivan Ramen's spicy red chili ramen, and Spice Symphony's chicken lollipops. So much for Domino's. The UberEATS website says, "Find what you're craving, and we'll handle the rest."

Uber was once a darling because of its unique model. Yet all is not well. Controversy continues to hound the company, showing that solutions must be presented ethically and fairly. The company faces criticism for its treatment of drivers, discrimination against certain passengers, sexual harassment of employees, and questionable use of customer information. Even in an Uber world, the most innovative solutions require execution with transparency and authenticity.

USE THE RIGHT BAIT

Marketing, when done right, matches the right customer with the right offer. It is relevant and it fits. It provides information. It meets a need and satisfies a want. Bill Bernbach, an icon of Madison Avenue who founded advertising agency DDB, said, "Be sure your advertising is saying something with substance, something that will inform and serve the consumer, and be sure you're saying it like it's never been said before."[18] Marketing that sells solutions provides that substance.

Informing and serving the consumer means making the solution relevant. The electronics company Acer learned this the hard way when it tested a new campaign, "Simplify My Life," in China. The campaign focused on the low price of its personal computers. This was a mistake, because to Chinese consumers, price is not as important as durability.[19]

Focus group participants found the low price suspicious. They were worried about performance and reliability. When Acer switched the marketing to emphasize those points, its market share doubled in less than two years. Acer learned what Dale Carnegie knew: "I am very fond of strawberries and cream, but I have found that for some strange reason, fish prefer worms. So when I went fishing, I didn't think about what I wanted. I thought about what they wanted. I didn't bait the hook with strawberries and cream. Rather, I dangled a worm or grasshopper in front of the fish."[20]

In my professional opinion, much of what is communicated by companies today is not salient, realistic, or relatable to actual lives. Amazon's Jeff Bezos has said, "What consumerism really is, at its worst, is getting people to buy things that don't actually improve their lives."[21] The lesson is simple: a product and its marketing must solve a problem. It helps when it makes people's lives easier, better, and more enjoyable.

Marketing has provided solutions to problems for a very long time. Archeologists recently discovered a wall painting dating back to 4200 BC. This ancient billboard has been studied and translated by experts who agree that the message on the wall reads, "Six ways a spear can save you from a wild boar."[22] The only thing missing from the mural is a website address. It provides a message of instruction and benefit. It must have prompted the reader to make a spear at the next opportunity. The wall painting marketed a solution.

You do not have to invent a razor or develop an innovative cracker package or disrupt the entire taxi industry to know that solutions work. This time-tested principle of marketing demands one thing: Whatever you provide, it stands a better chance of success if marketed as a solution. FedEx is an incredibly reliable and sophisticated logistics company but it actually sells peace of mind. This is reflected in successive taglines and marketing campaigns, such as, "When it absolutely, positively has to be there overnight," "Relax, it's FedEx," and "The world on time." The emphasis is on consistency and dependability. FedEx takes away shipping anxiety by emphasizing punctual delivery more than any other value. It is a solution to a practical need as well as to an emotional concern.

When presented as a solution, consumers more readily evaluate whether a product or service satisfies what they need or want. They decide if it will "fit" and solve something in their life. People expect to be marketed to, but they hate to be sold.

CHAPTER 2
MARKETING TELLS STORIES

"People think in stories, not statistics,
and marketers need to be master storytellers."[23]

ARIANNA HUFFINGTON, CO-FOUNDER, THE *HUFFINGTON POST*

When you meet someone for the first time or reconnect with an old friend or go to a dinner party, what takes place? You share an anecdote. You tell an old friend about what has been happening with your family and career since the last time you spoke. You talk to someone you've never met about your experiences and interests. In every case, you use storytelling to engage, connect and relate.

Storytelling helps us make sense of our lives and the world around us. It is an incredibly effective method of finding and sharing meaning and context. Mary Catherine Bateson, writer and cultural anthropologist, says, "The human species thinks in metaphors and learns through stories."[24] We are hardwired for stories because we have been telling them for centuries.

Stories inspire and motivate. Stories make ideas stick. Stories persuade. Stories educate and entertain. They are powerful because they can change people's minds and behavior.

One of the finest examples of storytelling in marketing drove the narrative for an entire industry. In 1912, a tenacious high school student, Edna Murphey, spotted an opportunity. Her father, a surgeon, had developed a liquid to keep his hands free of sweat while in the operating room.

Murphey thought the liquid might have another use, so she applied it to her armpits. It worked. She creatively named this new antiperspirant, Odorono ("Odor Oh No!"). The young entrepreneur convinced her family that she was on to something and borrowed $150 from her grandfather. The seed money funded a workshop for production and packaging. Murphey approached drugstores with Odorono but few expressed interest and those who did ended up returning unsold bottles.

Undeterred by these setbacks, Murphey moved the business to her parent's basement—as so many startups would do a century later. There she regrouped. The challenge was not with the product. It worked. The challenge was convincing people that perspiration was a problem. So Murphey reached out to advertising agency J. Walter Thompson.[25]

Thompson sent Murphey to James Webb Young, a fresh-faced copywriter who had once sold Bibles door-to-door. This training made Young well versed in the power of words and the need for persistence. He was just beginning his career but would later go on to lead J. Walter Thompson globally and be inducted into both the Creative Hall of Fame and the Advertising Hall of Fame.

Young's solution for Odorono was to attack commonly held beliefs about perspiration. At the time, people believed that preventing perspiration was unhealthy. Men were expected to have a husky scent and women did not address the topic of perspiration publicly. Most people tackled sweat and body odor privately by washing regularly and employing clothing shields.

Young devised a story focusing on the medicinal origins of Odorono. A modest campaign in magazines and stores created interest and soon people were taking Odorono seriously. Storeowners and salespeople had a story to tell and consumers an argument to consider. Sales climbed and Odorono's success launched Young's advertising career.

Within a few years revenues began to drop. Young was invited back to lift flagging sales. He commissioned a survey using the relatively new practice of market research. It revealed that women, two-thirds of the target market, found no use for deodorant. They were not persuaded by the health argument. These findings provided Young with a fresh insight that completely changed the perspiration conversation.

"Young decided to present perspiration as a social faux pas that nobody would *directly* tell you was responsible for your unpopularity, but which they were happy to gossip behind your back about."[26] The medicinal story line was replaced with one of social embarrassment.

An advertisement in an edition of *Ladies Home Journal* from 1919 launched the new narrative. The advertisement featured a sketch of a young couple resembling characters from *The Great Gatsby*. The well-dressed lovers are positioned in a close embrace that, for the time, was scandalous. But most of the impact came from the headline: "Within the curve of a women's arm. A frank discussion of a subject too often avoided." In other words it said, "If you want a romantic and passionate relationship then you had better not smell."[27]

The rest of the advertisement runs over 600 words. Young carefully selected each one to form an engrossing mix of inference, sermon, and solution. The story sets up the problem of embarrassing moisture and smell, provides product information countering any objection, and offers valuable dating and relationship advice. It is also lyrical: "A woman's arm! Poets have sung of it, great artists have painted its beauty. It should be the daintiest, sweetest thing in the world. And yet, unfortunately, it isn't always."[28]

This copy was blunt and the message was shocking for the time. The ad produced an indignant outcry from women who were insulted by the insinuation. But business results told a different story. According to J. Walter Thompson's archives, sales rose 112 percent. Young reinforced the story through another set of ads. One drew the reader in with this headline, "The most humiliating moment in my life when I overheard the cause of my unpopularity among men." It goes onto to normalize perspiring by saying it is "common to most of us." These messages read like earnest advice from a very direct friend.

Odorono extended its marketing to men. The company offered a free booklet called "The Assurance of Perfect Grooming," which covered male hygiene. More men-only deodorants hit the market in the 1930s. The brand names played off the social faux pas angle established by Young, with product names like Shun, Hush, Veto, and Perstop.[29]

Curiously, Odorono was not the first of its kind. The first trade-marked deodorant was Mum in 1888 followed 15 years later by the first trademarked antiperspirant, Everdry. But Odorono gets credit for writing the story of social embarrassment that has dominated the industry for over a hundred years. It turned out to be a very good business. The deodorant and antiperspirant industry is now worth more than $18 billion annually. Young's story was definitely a bestseller.

GET IT WRITE

We tell stories because they creatively and efficiently convey messages. A Native American proverb says: "Tell me the facts and I'll learn. Tell me the truth and I'll believe. But tell me a story and it will live in my heart forever." Storytelling is the oldest way to pass knowledge and a great way to connect brands and consumers.

In the television show *Mad Men*, creative director and Madison Avenue lothario Don Draper provides a quick lesson when a copywriter's words lack impact. Don says, "Stop writing for other writers."[30] The lesson is: put yourself in the shoes of the customer. Real life mad man Leo Burnett, eponymous creator of a great advertising firm, emphasized the same point: "If you can't turn yourself into your customer, you probably shouldn't be in the ad writing business at all."[31] Marketing stories have to be real, relevant, and relatable.

I am not a fan of overly simplistic stabs at marketing storytelling. Those attempts rob brands and businesses of what makes them interesting in the first place, namely, their depth and complexity. This does not mean every story should be *War and Peace,* but neither should marketing exist only as a tagline or a one-word association. I have struggled with this tension when penning marketing stories and have explored it with fellow professionals.

An insurance company got storytelling right almost a century ago. In the 1920s, Metropolitan Life sent out its famous "Penny in a Letter."[32] The goal was to remind people of the need to save for retirement. Inside every envelope was a real penny. That bit of extra weight inside the envelope ensured it would be opened. The letter challenged the reader to calculate how much they would have if they invested a penny a day for the next 25 years. At the time, that investment would generate more than $500, proving that a penny invested is interest earned. Finally, the letter asked readers to imagine what would happen if they put *more* than a penny aside.

This story compelled people to contact Metropolitan Life in unanticipated and unprecedented numbers. It was a creative way of getting people to think of their future and how Metropolitan Life could help. The "style was sober, as if writing to an existing customer—no sales-pitch hyperbole or advertising 'puff.'"[33] The letter was honest and helpful. It told a story of what could be and let people make up their own minds.

Storytelling is no easy business. Ask any writer with a manuscript on his hard drive or a published author looking to do it again. Chat honestly with an advertising copywriter or brand storyteller and they will quickly dispel the romantic view of writing. It is hard work.

STORIES THAT MOVE YOU

Mark Tungate is a British journalist and author based in Paris who focuses on media, branding, travel and lifestyle trends. He is a prolific writer whose books include *Luxury World: The Past Present and Future of Luxury Brands*, *Adland: A Global History of Advertising*, *Fashion Brands*, and *Branded Male*. Mark has also written for leading brands including Coca-Cola, MTV, and Diesel.

He is a firm believer that if you build a compelling story for a product or service, ultimately it will become attractive to the consumer. Mark told me about the marketing of Airbnb. This disruptive company is now in 191 countries and has accommodated over 400 million guests in other people's homes. Its marketing has leaned heavily on storytelling from its outset.

The hotel and resorts industry uses a marketing story that focuses on adventure and experiences. Over time, that message has lost its freshness. Airbnb positions itself as something different from hotels. Instead of marketing travel as an adventure, Airbnb has focused on the idea of belonging.

According to the company's co-founder and CEO Brian Chesky, "For so long, people thought Airbnb was about renting houses. But really, we're about home. You see, a house is just a space, but a home is where you belong. And what makes this global community so special is that for the very first time, you can belong anywhere. That is the idea at the core of our company: belonging."[34] This makes sense given the product is an exchange for renting other people's homes. Airbnb's initial storytelling helped convince people they would be comfortable in someone else's space.

One campaign's message was that Airbnb gives you what you can't get at the average hotel: someone else's view of the world. The narrator says, "I want you to feel at home here." It then takes the viewer through a variety of apartments, lofts, bungalows, and rural hideaways where the camera shoots through the dwelling's window to the outside. Unlike hotels, the facility is no longer the destination. Airbnb accommodations are a portal. The company reinforces that you are not staying in a place; you are part of the local community.

Mark explained that as Airbnb has grown and matured, so has its storytelling. In 2014, to mark the twenty-fifth anniversary of the fall of the Berlin Wall, the company created an integrated marketing campaign. At its heart was a one-minute animated story called "Wall and Chain." It depicts the true tale of two former border guards from East and West Berlin.

The emotional story begins in 1987 with a West German border guard. After completing his service, he leaves Berlin to settle in Denmark. But he is unable to reconcile his troubling experience as a border guard. His daughter plans a trip back to Berlin so he can see the positive changes in the city that have taken place. She books an apartment via Airbnb. On arrival, her father, the former guard, realizes that the person welcoming them to the apartment is, in fact, a guard from the east side of the wall. This meeting in a new era helps the former guard overcome the burden he had carried for so many years. In the animation, the character is literally chained to a section of the wall. He uses the key to the apartment to unlock himself.

The Airbnb ad is powerful visual storytelling. Mark said he believes it works because "the story changes the way people look at the world and how they can travel."

Airbnb is not always heavy in tone and content. In fact, the company has a lot of fun showing off its service and global reach. Airbnb has offered contests allowing winners to stay in very unique venues. One was an airplane parked at Schiphol Airport in Amsterdam. The plane was turned into an apartment with two bedrooms, multiple bathrooms, and Wi-Fi, and had a panoramic view from the cockpit. Another Airbnb contest let the winner stay overnight in an IKEA in Sydney, Australia. My favorite prize was a large ski gondola in Courchevel, France, that was converted into a bedroom for four. The winners arrived by snowmobile, enjoyed a regional dinner in the cable car, and a ride to the top of Saulire Mountain in the Alps. The following morning they were given first tracks on the slopes. For more storytelling, winners of all these contests were asked to share their stories of those exclusive and unique accommodations.

The company's central notion of belonging evolved further in April 2016. Airbnb rolled out a new brand campaign called "Live There." According to journalist Carolyn Said, "The company's goal is to persuade travelers that its far-flung network of homes provide experiences more intimate and more local than brands like Hilton or Sheraton. Its research shows that people use Airbnb because they 'want to live like a local,' the company said."[35]

This positioning tells both broad and personalized stories. It authentically connects masses of people to the local communities that they visit. This type of storytelling is dominating marketing today. You do not talk about the product, you describe the experience—that is more relevant and compelling.

WE ARE ALL CHARACTERS

Making the customer a primary character in the marketing story is a proven approach. So is creating characters that customers can identify with. Martin Conroy wrote a two-page advertisement for the *Wall Street Journal* that is one of the best examples of marketing storytelling ever. It is a modern parable. Conroy started his career as a copywriter for Bloomingdale's and moved to the editorial staff of *Esquire* magazine. He ended up at the advertising agency BBDO in 1950 where he counted General Electric, Sheraton, and Tupperware among his clients.

Conroy's famous "Two Young Men" story for the *Wall Street Journal* was a direct mail piece designed to sell subscriptions. The newspaper used it from 1975 to 2003, making it one of the longest continuously running direct mail marketing campaigns ever.[36] The piece has been credited with producing millions of dollars in subscription revenue.

The story is simple, uses homespun language, and carries a friendly, fairy tale quality. In the "Two Young Men" story, Conroy hit on exactly what the *Wall Street Journal* was selling. The story is told as if by the newspaper's publisher and was sent to prospective subscribers.

From its start, the story draws you in: "On a beautiful late spring afternoon, twenty-five years ago, two young men graduated from the same college. They were very much alike, these two young men. Both had been better than average students, both were personable and both—as young college graduates are—were filled with ambitious dreams for the future."

The story time travels to the future when the two men return to the college for their twenty-fifth reunion: "They were still very much alike. Both were happily married. Both had three children. And both, it turned out, had gone to work for the same Midwestern manufacturing company after graduation, and were still there. But there was a difference. One of the men was manager of a small department of that company. The other was its president."

So why was one more successful? What made the difference in their lives cannot be found in "native intelligence or talent or dedication" or in the fact that "one person wants success and the other person doesn't. The difference lies in what each person knows and how he or she makes use of that knowledge." That is when the letter gets to the point: ". . . the whole purpose of the *Journal*: to give its readers knowledge—knowledge that they can use in business."

The message was that the *Wall Street Journal* made you a success. What you learned and applied from its pages propelled your career. Direct marketing consultant James Rosenfield called the ad ". . . the 'Hamlet,' the 'Iliad,' the 'Divine Comedy' of direct-mail letters."[37] Alan Rosenspan, an expert in direct marketing, praised the letter: "I ask people to read out loud the first paragraph of the letter, and what's astonishing to me is that they never stop at the first paragraph. They keep on reading. And I tell them: 'You have just proven why this letter's so powerful. It's a story.'"[38]

On a trip to Morocco, I experienced firsthand the beauty of marketing as storytelling. I was invited to have tea with a group of rug merchants, to give them more time to persuade me to buy a $25,000 carpet I had repeatedly rejected. Over tea the men spoke eloquently of the carpet's origins. I was told it came from a historic

Berber village where it was lovingly hand-woven rather than knotted on old broad looms.

The rehearsed yet relaxed pitch went on to note that the carpet featured a one-of-a-kind geometric pattern. This was the reason for the value, as well as the richness of the natural vegetable dyes used. The men invited me into this story and then made me a part of it by asking, "Isn't twenty-five thosuand dollars reasonable for a rug that is incredibly beautiful and will last well over two hundred years?" This was great theater and I was entertained.

The gentlemen tried multiple narratives to convince me. They touched on resale value, pride of ownership, status, and memories of my current trip. I appreciated the effort but never considered seriously buying the carpet or even a modest alternative. When I told the rug merchants my wife would never, ever allow such a purchase, they promised they would find me a new wife! That prompted me to buy a much more reasonable cloth runner and end our storytelling session.

"Storytelling is the most powerful way to put ideas into the world today," says creative writing instructor Robert McKee.[39] He is widely known for his popular Story Seminar Series developed at the University of Southern California and is the author of *Story: Style, Structure, Substance, and the Principles of Screenwriting.* McKee consults on storytelling for Microsoft, Nike, Hewlett-Packard, and Siemens.

McKee has warned against the troubling trend of trying to simplify everything. Today, brief messaging is the norm in business communications. Marketers try to squish a complicated message into the length of a radio or television advertisement. Many TV ads are only ten seconds, and online they can be half that. We live in a world of texts and tweets. Two hundred eighty characters have become the norm and emojis are avatars for complex expression.

Marketers have responded by communicating in more frequent but shorter bursts.

Instead of the short and simple, I believe we should be celebrating complexity, because too often, simplifying only serves to dumb down the original idea. So if stories are, as McKee notes, the "currency of human contact,"[40] then they should be rich in development and telling.

The global financial institution HSBC has never shied away from the complex. Its marketing campaigns tackle subjects other organizations avoid. One headline from HSBC's 2012 "In the Future" campaign proclaims, "In the future, there will be no markets left waiting to emerge," and goes on to provide persuasive details. "By 2050, 19 of the 30 largest economies will be in countries we now call 'emerging'. HSBC's international network can help you discover new markets wherever they emerge next. There's a new world out there."[41]

Jennifer Aaker, a Stanford University marketing professor, has conducted studies that show stories are remembered up to 22 times more than facts alone.[42] Of course, great stories can be short or long. It is more a question of substance and depth. Richer storytelling represents an opportunity to differentiate in marketing.

Startup company Mailbox found a way to be different with its storytelling and the payoff was amazing. In 2013, technology company Dropbox acquired Mailbox and its e-mail management app for $100 million. What made this purchase extraordinary was the fact that the application was relatively simple and Mailbox had absolutely no revenue. Silicon Valley credited the high price to a one-minute video produced by Mailbox to share its tale.[43]

The video shows a young woman taking an afternoon off from work to go for a walk in the country. This outing does not mean she is untethered from the world, technology, or responsibilities because, thankfully, the Mailbox app is on her smartphone. Mailbox enables her to stay in touch, set meetings, and plan projects. Her fingers dance on the phone's screen and we witness how easy it is to use. She arranges her life efficiently and when finished, the phone is tucked into the back pocket of her jeans. She sets off light as air, knowing she can thoroughly enjoy her trek uninterrupted.

The video had no dialogue. No words appear over the images. All that accompanied the visuals was bouncy music. Still the message was abundantly clear. In order to experience and enjoy the real world, we have to arrange our online world. Mailbox could have loaded the video with facts and figures, graphs and charts. Instead, it demonstrated functionality and benefit through a story.

STORIES THAT DON'T SELL

Marketing increasingly resembles the entertainment industry. In 1988, David Ogilvy, known as the "Father of Advertising," reflected on how the profession had changed. He voiced concern that advertising had become simple amusement: ". . . the people who do it have absolutely no interest in selling anything. They think of themselves as entertainers and geniuses. In the end the entertainment gets in the way of the message, thwarting its real purpose."[44] This was anathema to the man who had once stated in his book, *Confessions of an Advertising Man*, "I do not regard advertising as entertainment or an art form, but as a medium of information."[45]

Storytelling can and should entertain, but in the case of marketing, its purpose is to make consumers aware of a product, compel them to try it, keep them coming back, and tell others about it. That means the marketer has to make sure he or she understands a consumer's motives and that the story told provides an honest justification to buy.

Two of the most popular marketing campaigns of the twentieth century offered great entertainment but were sales flops. The first debuted in 1969. It was the famous "Spicy Meatball" television commercial for Alka-Seltzer. It is held up by the marketing industry as incredibly clever and creative. And it is. The ad actually lampoons advertising by showing an actor making a series of mistakes as he is filmed for a commercial.

This irreverent commercial-within-a-commercial features the increasingly exasperated actor promoting an unnamed spicy meat sauce. The poor guy cannot get his line right. "That's a spicy meat-a-ball!" is said over and over, accompanied each time by a bite of meatball. The scene is shot so many times and so many meatballs are consumed that the actor suffers from indigestion. This prompts the need for Alka-Seltzer. It is undeniably a fun concept and cute little story.

During its fifty-second run time, only seven seconds show an Alka-Seltzer bottle. The name "Alka-Seltzer" appears on screen for a few seconds at the end. The "spicy meat-a-ball" line became a part of pop culture. But the commercial backfired. The nondescript jar of meat sauce sat on the table for almost the entire commercial. People assumed the spot was advertising the pasta sauce, not Alka-Seltzer. Sales for the antacid and pain reliever were static while numerous pasta sauces flew off the shelves. The ad entertained but did not sell.[46]

In the 1990s, the Taco Bell Chihuahua spokesdog seemed to be everywhere. The money spent to support the tiny animal was impressive. The dog was a pop culture success. Toy figures and other merchandise were sold and the line, "*¡Yo quiero Taco Bell!*" ("I want Taco Bell!") was widely quoted. So it was suspicious when the company yanked the campaign in 2000. Speculation included the death of the actual animal.

The real reason for the removal of the ads: Taco Bell had experienced a six percent drop in sales since the campaign began.[47] The marketing appeared successful but the business results were not. An executive from rival Wendy's replaced the president of Taco Bell and the advertising agency was fired. Entertaining marketing stories do not necessarily grow sales, and in some cases, can drive consumers away.

When storytelling becomes trite or copycat, it loses its effectiveness. Let's look what has happened to marketing in the insurance industry. Historically, fear was the primary motive employed to convince consumers to purchase health, life, car, and home insurance. The idea was to scare people into protecting themselves.

Over time, fear became ineffective. Doom and gloom repelled consumers. So the industry turned to humor. This was not a bad idea, given that people recall humorous tales. According to Millward Brown, a brand research consultancy, half of all advertisements on television use humor.[48] This is why we have seen leading insurers using a gecko, a duck, a quirky saleswoman, a knowledgeable but gruff professor, and a character named "Mayhem."

Allstate created Mayhem to act as a mischievous metaphor for potential disasters. The scenarios Mayhem produces place consumers in difficult situations to motivate them to buy insurance on the chance such events would occur. Mayhem initiates scary situations but the humorous approach tempers any real fear. Winston Churchill said, "A joke is a very serious thing."

The marketing by Geico, AFLAC, Progressive Insurance, Farmer's Insurance, and Allstate all draw from the same source, using irreverence and metaphor rather than stark statistics regarding risk in our lives. The companies have pursued the same strategy in the same way. They are successful, but they end up battling for small gains in market share versus category leadership. It is an industry characterized by high customer churn. The marketing generates laughs and incremental sales. I believe it is an industry that needs a fresh perspective.

What makes storytelling succeed or fail to market a product? Storytelling fails when the tellers are too focused on themselves. A story succeeds when it prompts the recipient to change thinking and behavior. This requires a marketer to be both storyteller and psychologist. Marketers have to give people a reason to believe, a way to connect, and justification for making a purchase.

THIS ONE, NOT THAT ONE

Marketers in the apparel industry are often brilliant storytellers. They provide motives and justifications for the purchase even when those purchases are budget busters. The apparel brand Lacoste is an instructive example of the benefits of creating excitement and celebrity interest in a product. René Lacoste was not only a fine tennis player, he was also a keen observer. Before the 1920s, men playing tennis wore long-sleeved, button-down shirts that restricted movement. Lacoste spotted the Marquis of Cholmondeley playing in a polo shirt.[49] The style allowed flexibility and comfort. After retiring from competitive tennis, Lacoste started his clothing business using the polo shirt as differentiator. The business was a modest success but could not break into the United States.

Though Lacoste's product was positioned as "the status symbol of the competent sportsman," it failed to compel the 1950s American consumer to part with eight dollars for a shirt. The company had a problem. The Lacoste brand was premium, foreign, and unfamiliar. How could it convince Americans to wear the alligator instead of other popular clothing symbols such as the penguin from Munsingwear or the sheep suspended in a ribbon from Brooks Brothers? The brand was caught in a challenging marketing dilemma. They couldn't push the product and they couldn't get consumers to pull.

It turns out the best way to break into the United States was to leverage American symbols. The 1950s was a time of burgeoning abundance, and the United States was leading the way. Americans were living a better life. Lascoste sent shirts, sweaters, and other garments free of charge to presidents John F. Kennedy and Dwight D. Eisenhower, along with other influential Americans. *Life* and *Time* magazines featured photographs of Bing Crosby in a Lacoste cardigan sweater golfing and enjoying a nineteenth-hole cocktail.[50]

The Lacoste campaign personified the ideals of the market it wanted to reach. People wore an alligator above their left breast because it came to symbolize success in America. Demand for the clothing forced department stores to carry the Lacoste line.

In the case of a brand, the story is never completely told. The constant interactions with consumers breathe fresh air into the tale. This is why brands reinvent and retool with ever-greater frequency. I have clients who have overhauled their brand three times in ten years. In the past, this would be criticized as frivolous, evidence of inaccurate branding in the first place, or just plain wrong. Today, these can be fresh chapters in a brand's ongoing and evolving story.

CHAPTER 3

MARKETING LEVERAGES EMOTION

"Good advertising does not just circulate information. It penetrates the public mind with desires and belief."[51]

LEO BURNETT, FOUNDER, LEO BURNETT WORLDWIDE

Plato wrote, "Human behavior flows from three main sources: desire, emotion, and knowledge." Plato would have made a fine marketer. The three sources he identifies are foundational to marketing. People's desires start the entire process. Businesses are built to satisfy what people crave and require. Emotion has been proven to be powerful in marketing. It helps produce a reaction and make a more personal connection. Information is needed so a consumer can make a smart choice. Emotion compellingly conveys that information.

In 1999, *Advertising Age* produced a ranking of the top ten slogans of the twentieth century.[52] It included "Just do it" for Nike, "We try harder" for Avis, and "Does she . . . or doesn't she?" for Clairol. The number one slogan was De Beers's "A diamond is forever." It is an emotional message that has been in use since 1947.

When De Beers tried to break into the American market in 1938, most people thought an engagement ring was an indulgence. People were just recovering from the Depression and money was still so tight that only ten percent of engagement rings contained diamonds. The ad's copywriter, Frances Gerety, said that people spent money on "a washing machine, or a new car, anything but an engagement ring. It was considered just absolutely money down the drain."[53] The N.W. Ayer ad agency set out "to create a situation where almost every person pledging marriage feels compelled to acquire a diamond engagement ring."[54]

The agency positioned the diamond engagement ring as the physical symbol of love and commitment. This was easier said than done. Consumers were aware that diamond rings depreciated by at least fifty percent the moment they left the jewelry store. (As a comparison, a new car loses about nine percent of value when it leaves the lot.)

An N.W. Ayer memo from the early days of its relationship with De Beers reads, "Sentiment is essential to your advertising, as it is to your product, for the emotional connotation of the diamond is the one competitive advantage which no other product can claim or dispute." In other words, emotion was the point of differentiation.

"A Diamond Is Forever" crystallized the sentiment that a diamond, like a loving relationship, is forever. Between 1939 and 1979, De Beers's sales in the United States increased from $23 million to $2.1 billion.[55] N.W. Ayer had turned an expensive purchase into a necessity for bride and groom. The 1951 annual report for N.W. Ayer reported on this trend: "For a number of years we have found evidence that the diamond engagement ring tradition is consistently growing stronger. Jewelers now tell us 'a girl is not engaged unless she has a diamond engagement ring.'"

De Beers reported that consumers spent $41 billion on diamond jewelry in the United States in 2016, up from $39 billion in 2015.[56] But now there is a new challenge. Industry analysts indicate that retail sales of diamonds are slowing. It appears the millennial generation is not as interested in diamonds, and might choose other gemstones or synthetic diamonds if and when they marry at all.[57]

The Jewelers of America, an 8,000-member trade association, and the Diamond Producers Association, representing seven of the world's leading diamond producers, have taken note. In 2016, the Diamond Producers Association began an advertising campaign directed at millennials with the slogan, "Real is rare, real is a diamond." The association's CEO, Jean-Marc Lieberherr, said, "what underpins the 'real is rare' strategy . . . is to connect at a deep emotional level with millennials, who are an important group now. That's the biggest generation in the US and within a few years they'll be the biggest consuming generation. They are also the generation getting married, and the bridal or kind of romantic engagement cachet is still the cornerstone of this industry."[58]

I LOVE MY VACUUM

Marketing works when it makes us feel something. From a psychological perspective, when we feel strongly about something, we are pushed to action. Emotions help drive buying decisions and then our logic works to justify them.

Iain Ellwood is the Chief Growth Officer at Group XP, a consultancy that provides customer experience innovation. Iain has worked with Bank of America, British Airways, InterContinental Hotels, Mercedes-Benz, and Virgin, and is the author of five books on branding and marketing. When I spoke with Iain, he used the example of Dyson to discuss leveraging emotion to market products. Said Iain, "I have come to the conclusion that emotion-based marketing is the only effective way to market because it offers benefits to both the customers and the company. It is about making the customer feel special. If we make customers feel special, they'll pay almost any price for that feeling. Dyson is a great example where they have doubled or tripled the value or price of a product."

Dyson designs appliances such as vacuum cleaners, hand dryers, bladeless fans, and heaters. The company had revenues of over $4.8 billion in 2017.[59] Iain said he believes the company has grown by creating emotional connections. "Dyson has made people feel special about cleaning the house again. They have created an emotional benefit for the consumer. Unless we make people feel something, we can't expect them to be attracted to a brand. Emotions drive our primary decisions, therefore we buy things that make us feel something."

Iain noted other brands where emotion guides the marketing: "Nike has built an entire business on making people feel like athletes, even though they mostly sit on the couch. Nike has shrewdly understood this valuable, nuanced insight. Disney is a brand that makes you feel like a child again. In a heavily mortgaged, adult, stressful world, having an attitude of childlike wonder is absolutely priceless."

Brands are relationships and every relationship runs on some kind of emotional connection. Iain told me he believes emotional marketing "gets to those implicit feelings quicker. Successful marketers understand which emotions may work on an immediate, intuitive level more than a layered, thoughtful process of customer decision making."

But back to vacuum cleaners. How are emotions attached to a Dyson purchase? Iain postulated that Dyson has cleverly tapped into the male emotions in the purchase of a vacuum cleaner. "When you look at all Dyson's products, their aesthetic is very masculine and performance-driven. They're not girlish with feminine colors.

This is common today in product design. Baby strollers now look like techno SUVs because brands recognize that men are getting more involved in buying these household goods. This aesthetic allows them to still feel masculine whilst buying and using what is a domestic product. They are tapping into the machismo of male consumers while providing the status of having the 'fastest car on the road' in vacuum cleaners. These are two very clear higher-order emotional benefits."

I SECOND THAT EMOTION

Coca-Cola has spent 130 years making its brand synonymous with happiness. And what's a happier image than Santa Claus? According to the company's website, Santa was first paired with Coke for an advertisement in the December 1930 issue of *The Saturday Evening Post*.[60] The ad shows kids admiring a department store Santa Claus who is enjoying a glass of the cola.

A year later the D'Arcy advertising agency developed a series of images envisioning the life of the "real" Santa Claus rather than a department store version. They mined Clement Clark Moore's 1822 poem, "A Visit From St. Nicholas," which begins with the famous line, "'Twas the night before Christmas."[61] Over the years, Coca-Cola's Santa reviews lists, delivers toys, eats treats, and visits children, always while enjoying a Coke. Santa became a seasonal celebrity for the brand, gracing store displays, billboards, posters, and calendars.

Robert Woodruff was president of the company from 1923 to 1954. Under his leadership, Coke moved from away from selling a soft drink to selling an idea. That concept seems to have driven Coca-Cola's culture of "happiness" ever since.

The D'Arcy advertising agency helped drive Coca-Cola's optimistic and positive tone all year round. They focused the marketing on the pleasure Coke delivered.

Illustrations from Norman Rockwell and N. C. Wyeth from the 1920s and 1930s helped people visualize the joy of Coke in their daily lives. Wyeth's paintings featured Huckleberry Finn-like characters carrying fishing rods and Cokes. Every illustration by Wyeth for Coke suggests simple enjoyment and fulfillment.

Rockwell's work told more layered emotional stories. One advertisement shows a keen young man in a suit delivering a tray of Cokes to a company vice president. This suggested Coke was one of the benefits of hard work and accomplishment: drinking Coke signaled success and achievement. Another depicts two young suburban couples enjoying a groomed backyard and chilled Cokes. The message of this ad is clear: happiness and the good life come with Coca-Cola.

Coca-Cola has had 46 tag lines in 130 years, including: "Enjoy Thirst," "Makes Good Things Taste Better," "Have a Coke and a Smile," "You Can't Beat the Feeling," and "Open Happiness."[62] Each slogan seeks to resonate emotionally with consumers. They all reference a positive emotion or allude to happiness.

In January 2016, Coca-Cola announced that for the first time, all of the company's beverage brands would be united in one global creative campaign called "Taste the Feeling."[63] The tagline connotes the idea that drinking a Coca-Cola product is a simple pleasure that makes everyday moments more special. Chief Marketing Officer Marcos de Quinto said, "We want to help remind people why they love the product as much as they love the brand."[64]

Rodolfo Echeverria, Vice President of Global Creative, Connections and Digital at Coca-Cola, avoided calling this a campaign or set of ads. He referred to them as "emotional product communications."[65] The company is using emotional storytelling and showcasing moments people share while drinking Coke. The company is going right for the emotional jugular by telling stories of first dates, first kisses, and first loves. Clearly, Coca-Cola remains committed to communicating and selling happiness.

HAPPY OR SAD, YOU WILL FIND IT IN AN AD

Marketing depends on the right emotion and on the right message. Some brands use inspirational stories that explore a range of emotions. These stories are profound, real, and life changing. They use affection, angst, courage, embarrassment, fear, guilt, jealousy, pride, and sadness.

Since there has been advertising, there have been emotional advertisements. I still remember one that, at the tender of age of six, caused me to feel sad and angry. *Advertising Age* recognized it as one of the top 100 advertising campaigns of the twentieth century. It was for the nonprofit organization Keep America Beautiful and was launched on Earth Day 1971.

Called "The Crying Indian," the one-minute public service announcement featured a Native American man paddling a canoe in a pristine river. As he progresses, we see that the water is polluted. The man surveys it all with a weathered face and stoic expression. He beaches the canoe on a shore littered with garbage. On a neighboring highway cars rush by spewing exhaust. A car window opens and a bag of fast-food trash explodes at the man's feet. A voice-over asks Americans to stop littering and polluting. The camera pans to the man's cheerless face. Dramatically, a single tear rolls down his cheek.

This advertisement "secured two Clio awards, incited a frenzy of community involvement, and helped reduce litter by 88 percent across 38 states. Its star performer, a man who went by the name 'Iron Eyes Cody,' subsequently became the 'face of Native Indians,' and was honored with a star on Hollywood's Walk of Fame. Advertisers estimate that his face, plastered on billboards, posters, and magazine ads, has been viewed fourteen billion times, easily making him the most recognizable Native American figure of the century."[66] (A curious side note: Cody was Italian, not Native American. But that's another story.)

Consumers make buying decisions based on how they feel. In his book, *Emotional Design: Why We Love (or Hate) Everyday Things*, cognitive scientist Donald Norman explains, "Everything we do, everything we think is tinged with emotion, much of it subconscious. In turn, our emotions change the way we think, and serve as constant guides to appropriate behavior, steering us away from the bad, guiding us toward the good."[67]

Norman wrote an earlier book, *The Design of Everyday Things*, in 1980. But in the prologue to *Emotional Design*, written in 2004, Norman confessed that in the earlier book, "I didn't take emotions into account. I addressed utility and usability, function and form, all in a logical, dispassionate way—even though I am infuriated by poorly designed objects. But now I've changed. Why? In part because of new scientific advances in our understanding of the brain and of how emotion and cognition are thoroughly intertwined. We scientists now understand how important emotion is to everyday life, how valuable. Sure utility and usability are important, but without fun and pleasure, joy and excitement, and yes, anxiety and anger, fear and rage, our lives would be incomplete."[68]

Most people do not believe marketing can influence them. They have faith that their rational mind is in control. But it is not—at least, not entirely. Matt Eastwood is Global Chief Creative Officer for the advertising agency JWT. On the subject of emotion

MARKETING LEVERAGES EMOTION | 47

in marketing and emotional connection between brands and consumers, Matt quoted Maya Angelou: "I've learned that people will forget what you said, people will forget what you did, but people will never forget how you made them feel."

Matt said, "In dealing with so many different client organizations, they're often quite desperate to talk about what they consider to be their unique product differentiation, or the logical message that they want to communicate to customers. But it's not the product's uniqueness, it's the way you make customers feel unique. That emotion, in a world where products are at parity, is the only differentiator between two different brands or products."

Matt mentioned his work with Johnson & Johnson to illustrate this point. The company's McNeil consumer products business had recalled Tylenol and other over-the-counter products in 2010 because of quality lapses. Eastwood explained, "Tylenol was taken off the shelf because they found foreign substances in the bottles and it completely damaged the brand. Sales plummeted sixty percent. It became our job to reintroduce the brand. We started with a classic discussion of efficacy and efficiency. Eventually we agreed that we had to address it differently. What Tylenol actually offers is health for your family. So we did a whole campaign under the hashtag '#HowWeFamily.'"

Matt described the campaign: "It was a demonstration of what the modern family is like today. We profiled mixed-race families, same-sex families, divorced parents. But the most interesting thing to me about the campaign is that there is no product shot at all. There is no one taking Tylenol. There is no 'efficacy story.' It is all emotion.

"The first piece we did was at Thanksgiving and was based on Norman Rockwell's painting of that holiday called 'Freedom from Want.' It depicts a large family about to carve the turkey. We re-imagined that family setting in different ways. We featured a Japanese family, an African-American family headed by a grandmother, and a blended family that included a lesbian couple. It included a voice-over from Rockwell's granddaughter, Abigail Rockwell, who talked about how he would have seen family today and who would have been in that kind of idyllic American painting.

"It got such a positive reaction on Twitter and Facebook. People said, 'This is what a brand should be about.' And the sales have recovered. You can use all the logic in the world but you must make an emotional connection with people. That's what we did, and it reinvigorated the brand."

Matt recognized that consumers were willing to forgive Tylenol. "There was forgiveness because J&J has portrayed itself as a family brand for a long, long time. We had to remind people that the company cares." This was made somewhat easier because Johnson & Johnson has long invested in brand loyalty and built a stockpile of capital with consumers. Chris Malone, chief advisory officer of Relational Capital Group, wrote in the *Harvard Business Review*, "Companies like J&J, who understand how consumers judge brands, can build intense customer loyalty that withstands even the most difficult crisis. Consciously or otherwise, they know that brand relationships at their root are like human relationships – so they act accordingly."[69]

EMOTION CONVEYS AND CONNECTS

In marketing, it is not a contest between emotion and logic. Marketing uses emotion to convey logic and information. People engage with emotion and then they weigh the arguments and absorb the information emotion carries. The Dove "Real Beauty" marketing campaign is a great example of the power of emotion when combined with logic. It evoked a strong emotional response from both supporters and detractors.

Unilever owns Dove and scores of other beauty product brands. The "Real Beauty" campaign garnered consumer, media, and marketing industry attention because it attempted to change the entire beauty conversation. The mission was, "To make women feel comfortable in the skin they are in, to create a world where beauty is a source of confidence and not anxiety."[70] Instead of women attempting to change their appearance, "Real Beauty" asked them to be comfortable with their bodies whether they were old or young, fat or thin.

The catalyst for the "Real Beauty" campaign was a study conducted in 2002 by Unilever's public relations firm, Edelman. It surveyed "more than 3,000 women in ten countries in order to learn about women's priorities and interests. When it reported that only two percent of the women interviewed considered themselves beautiful, the executives at Dove saw an opportunity."[71]

It was a brave choice. Dove started a conversation without knowing where it would lead. The campaign began modestly to assess reaction with "tick box" billboards that debuted in Canada in 2004 and eventually spread to the United States and the United Kingdom. The billboards featured photographs of women with two options printed next to them, such as "Fat or fit?" and "Withered or wonderful?" People texted their vote to a listed number and the results appeared on the billboard. It created interest and drove 1.5 million people to the Campaign for Real Beauty website.[72]

Months later, Dove attracted even more media and public attention with a fresh billboard campaign, showing groups of diverse women in their underwear. Not many campaigns get the advertising industry buzzing in admiration and jealousy, but "Real

Beauty" did just that. It dominated water cooler, lunch, and martini chats. It was featured at every marketing conference and in every trade publication.

Dove's campaign continued with a series of short films. "Daughters" featured interviews with mothers and their daughters discussing their relationships. "Onslaught" looked at how the beauty industry targets young girls. "Evolution" revealed how makeup and digital alterations make an average woman unnaturally look like a supermodel. That particular film has been viewed on YouTube over nineteen million times.

Pundits argued that the campaign was hypocritical. In addition to Dove, Unilever sells Slimfast, Axe, and Fair & Lovely skin-whitening cream. People wondered if Unilever could authentically lead the beauty debate, given the fact that it profits from these kinds of cosmetic products.[73] And there was significant criticism that the ads continued the old standard of women judging themselves based on appearance, rather than "intelligence and wit and ethical sensibility, not just our faces and bodies."[74]

But from a marketing perspective, the campaign was a success. It was named the best campaign of the first fifteen years of the twenty-first century by *Advertising Age*. Dove sales now top $4 billion annually, compared with $2.5 billion when the campaign started.[75]

EMOTION IS CURRENCY

John Allert, group brand director of McLaren Technology Group, the iconic British Formula One racing team and supercar manufacturer, discussed with me the importance of emotion in marketing. "Emotion is our basic unit of currency. We are a brand founded on the aspiration or ambition of winning, which for us is really a quest to prevail in everything we do. That is innately emotional and resonates with people who buy into the idea of overcoming adversity, or triumphing, or prevailing. That's obviously credible to our sport and to our road car products, but it's very much true of everything we do. We exist to win. People enjoy a brand that has that level of ambition, and, I suspect, probably see part of that in themselves."

The ambition of winning injects life into the McLaren brand. That makes it more relatable and relevant to the customers the company wishes to attract. The values and attributes of a brand tend to mirror those of its most desired customer. It is a form of self-expression.

All sorts of emotional content can create a great commercial. Comfort and reassurance are what spaghetti sauce brand Ragu strove for in a 2012 campaign. Mike Dwyer, US foods director of Ragu's parent company, Unilever, observed, "It can be tough being a kid. And when it's tough being a kid, mom and dad want to comfort their kids and the way they do that is through meal time, and Ragu sits squarely in that space."[76]

The campaign depicted a range of scenarios where kids encountered tough times only to be comforted by a spaghetti dinner. These scenarios draw from real life moments. A mother uses her saliva to clean a spot of sauce off her child's embarrassed face. A father assures his daughter that the perky hamster is the same pet that had been recently ailing.

The marquee spot of the campaign attracted a lot of attention. It portrayed that horrific moment when a child walks in on the parents in a very intimate situation. Dwyer believed the ads created a connection through familiarity. He said, "The key is you have an insight that you can tap into that people go, 'Oh yeah, I've been there.'"[77]

But sometimes, powerful emotions can drive customers away. Causes have often leaned on guilt and shame to gain attention. The mission of the World Wide Fund for Nature is "Building a future in which people live in harmony with nature." Over the last several years, this conservation organization has grown in influence and now touts over five million supporters and five thousand staff members. It also has a serious marketing budget. But much of what it communicates is a downer. I am struck by the way the marketing tells people they should feel extremely guilty for the state of our world.

This is the same strategy that was used by the Christian Children's Fund in the 1970s. That organization's ads were ubiquitous for the better part of a decade. They featured sad, malnourished children while spokesperson Sally Struthers spoke with a mopey direness. In my opinion, the commercials were preachy, judgmental, and downright depressing. People began to change the channel as they became inured to the campaign's depressing imagery and message.

The World Wide Fund for Nature is repeating the same mistake. The marketing has always been professional, but the goal is to jar people. One print ad shows a woman with a roller suitcase walking through an airport. The suitcase is leaving a blood trail. It reads, "Don't buy exotic animal souvenirs." Another series shows various endangered animals covered in graffiti with the question, "What will it take before we respect the planet?"

The Advertising Standards Authority in the United Kingdom issued a report in 2012 on advertising by charities. It found that the sector produced some of the most offensive ads. The report stated, "Many participants felt that some charity adverts contained offensive content that went too far in seeking to make people feel uncomfortable or guilty, or used imagery that was considered too distressing despite being for a worthwhile cause."[78]

I believe the messaging for these causes should tap hope, not guilt. Too often in its advertising, the World Wide Fund for Nature seems to have forgotten that it exists to make change and share victories. Instead, it lectures and chastises while it asks for money. It needs to give people something to believe in, show how their work is paying off, and celebrate success. It needs to show gratitude to their supporters. Hope and progress would go farther than shame and shock. Then they may be able to spend less on marketing, fundraising and administration.

Andy Wilson, head of strategy at advertising agency BBDO Asia Pacific, made clear the link between marketing and emotion: "The essential difference between emotion and reason is that emotion leads to action while reason leads to conclusion. And this is why creative work for brands should be focused on triggering emotion responses."[79]

Emotion taps into people's desires. We all make buying decisions based on how we feel. The goal of emotion in marketing is to make people feel something while delivering the information needed to make the best possible decision.

CHAPTER 4
MARKETING BUILDS RELATIONSHIPS

"We are all emotional beings looking for
relevance, context, and connection."[80]

BETH COMSTOCK, VICE CHAIR OF BUSINESS INNOVATIONS, GENERAL ELECTRIC

According to an article in the *Harvard Business Review*, "Acquiring a new customer is anywhere from five to 25 times more expensive than retaining an existing one."[81] Strong, mutually beneficial relationships with customers yield a host of benefits. Achieving a customer's absolute loyalty to a brand and maintaining it is nearly impossible, though; preference is a more reasonable goal.

When customers treat one brand preferentially, they are less price-conscious and will spend more with that brand. Such customers are also more likely to share positive word-of-mouth. Having happy customers produces an ironic benefit. Contented customers tend to purchase your products with less marketing required. That may be the ultimate goal of marketing: not having to market. On a relative basis, Starbucks and Apple spend less money on traditional advertising for this very reason.

So why doesn't every company just flat-out focus on creating longstanding relationships? Many companies do. But maintaining relationships is tough stuff. Psychologist, sociologist, and social researcher Hugh Mackay summed up the difficulty. "Nothing is perfect," he wrote. "Life is messy. Relationships are complex. Outcomes are uncertain. People are irrational."[82]

LVMH is a company that sells luxury brands such as Veuve Clicquot champagne and Louis Vuitton fashion. According to Damien Vernet, president of LVMH Asia, the relationship with the customer is paramount. Vernet says, "The goal is not to sell a bag; it is to build a relationship of confidence and trust with the customer."[83] But building relationships is easier said than done. Take the case of a slim piece of chocolate.

In 1962, After Eight mints debuted in England. The thin square treats have a mint core covered in dark chocolate. Each comes in its own little pouch. The product name, with its accompanying clock logo, tells people when to enjoy the mints—after eight o'clock in the evening. This was new social entertaining information in the early 1960s, when socializing mostly meant a beer at the local pub.

The product came at the right time. The austerity measures that had gripped the country following the Second World War were disappearing. Growing stability and affluence meant the return of sophisticated socializing. After Eight's initial marketing offered advice on how to throw a successful dinner party. Print advertisements showed couples around elaborate tables that had been the scene of an impressive meal. The people were well dressed. The setting communicated refinement. Everyone was enjoying each other's company while enjoying a box of mints.

The dinner party became the focal point and the mints played a supporting role. This was a classic soft sell. It was a subtle, casual, and friendly sales message. It presents an implied conclusion with associated benefits. In other words, consumers could see themselves in this picture. This was what the marketing of After Eight mints was out to accomplish—that social instruction with cachet would nurture mint sales over the long term.

The marketing suggested the mints represented a better and "richer" life. In the first After Eight television commercial, the hostess states, "I may be old-fashioned, but I like leaving the men to drink their coffee. It means we can abscond with the After Eights." The ad communicates social status and cultural refinement. From the start, consumers responded to what the product offered. They never took it too seriously, but they identified with the ideal it posed.[84]

Later campaigns shifted to highlight glamour. The scenes and subjects were suave, debonair, and polished. A magazine advertisement featured an elegantly dressed hostess with the copy, "Nowadays our guests expect After Eights." The message was clear. People who ended dinner parties with After Eight mints achieved higher social standing.

Then came a problem. After Eight encountered two marketing challenges as the business grew. The product's premise was based on eating the mints later in the evening following a dinner. This cut out many hours of possible consumption and limited sales. The next problem was that the mints were to be purchased by the dinner party hosts and served to guests. That limited the market. Constrained consumption and a restricted market were barriers to growth.

After Eight refined its marketing to increase sales opportunities. Instead of the hosts buying and offering the mints post-dinner, fresh campaigns suggested that buying After Eight mints as a gift for the hostess would build their own social cachet. This idea was meant to double or triple sales. It was no faux pas if multiple guests arrived, each bearing a box of After Eights as a gift. And they did.

The advertisements continued to portray people socializing, but now they did it at lunch, tea, cocktails, and even while driving.

No longer would people have to wait until after eight. A print advertisement from the late 1960s featured two stylish women in a Ferrari. One is complaining about having to source a unique delicacy for her husband. It used delightfully quirky copy: "It's the only way I manage to survive in London traffic. I mean, here we are, stuck in this ridiculous jam, trying to find someone who sells Charle's Yak Stew or whatever it was he wanted and were it not for these delectable Thin Mints I should be . . . Cynthia! You, you snake! You've eaten them all."

In the 1980s the company recognized that the brand needed to broaden its appeal. After Eight marketing had been ignoring lower-income consumers. In order to attract them, the mint marketers chose self-deprecation to poke fun at After Eights' implied exclusivity. This was a gamble, but more consumers responded and it did not alienate existing ones. Everyone identified with the tongue-in-cheek intent and sentiment. The company accomplished this with a campaign of invented words that defined the ways people consume After Eights.

The word "Cholmond" referred to the removal of a single mint from the box without removing the tiny envelope it came in. "Cholmonding" was said to be "much frowned upon in polite society." "Grebbling" dealt with the raised relief pattern found on the surface of the mint. In proper company, "the grebbling should always face outwards." Meanwhile "sweaving" gave people license to eat the mints any way they wanted, at any time and in any quantity.

After Eight's marketing has a familiar cycle. For a period of time, it set rules for proper social convention; in the next period, it challenged those rules humorously. More recent ads hearken back to the original marketing that provides social instruction. It contains a photo of one of the square mints and the copy reads, "If you want a great dinner party, don't cut corners." Once again consumers are told that successful entertaining hinges on a box of mints.

This cycle has endeared the brand to consumers for decades. After Eight is still the leading chocolate mint treat in the world. It has that distinction by being true to itself, evolving the communications while maintaining and endearing self-deprecation, and leveraging decades of nostalgia. The buyers of After Eight mints are following in the footsteps of their parents.

BUILDING A RELATIONSHIP

Niraj Dawar is a professor in marketing at the Ivey Business School at the University of Western Ontario. His research focuses on brand equity, consumer's use of brand, and consumer behavior.

Niraj told me, "We get all mushy about the customer relationship, but fundamentally the reason to build a relationship is to lower the cost of transactions and make it easier for the customer to identify the reasons and the rationale to buy. That is the basis of the relationship." He could be describing After Eight mints.

Niraj gave an example of the difference between selling individual automobiles and selling automobile leases. "These transactions are very different in terms of how the company approaches a sale, what they know about the customer, and how they benefit from that relationship over a period of time. When you sell a car, you sell the individual unit, and then you expect the customer to come back six or seven years later. You never know what the customer is up to during that period of time. Does he like the car? Is he thinking about buying other cars?"

But leasing is different. "With a lease," said Niraj, "everything changes. You are in a monthly contract with the buyer, you know when the lease will expire, you know what the end date is, you know when to market to the buyer, you know how to engender and foster loyalty to the buyer through car servicing. The purpose of the channel, of the dealership, of the financing, of the billing relationship that you have—it's very different in a leasing model than in a single sale. And this model is now pervading all sorts of products."

The subscription model (e. g., a lease) provides greater opportunity to know the customer and deepen the relationship. "Customer preferences over time provide information that is invaluable. It is only possible to know consumers if you have a direct relationship with them. Subscription models and direct relationships are undermining the claim of traditional models that have always sold within a channel and through two or three levels of intermediaries. Companies that have the direct relationship learn and serve customers in a much deeper way than has traditionally been the case."

In marketing relationships, the marketer's goal is to make a brand both a need and a want. That means knowing the customer so well that the product or service becomes a desire that must be satisfied again and again.

RELATIONSHIPS ARE AS DELICATE AS CHINA

Maintaining an ongoing relationship with customers is not a new concept. Josiah Wedgwood, who founded his china company in 1759, not only created practical and precious products, he knew how to position them as a necessity. The Wedgwood company has practiced sophisticated marketing for centuries to create strong customer relationships.

Long before these tactics became familiar practice, Wedgwood used market segmentation, prestige pricing, style obsolescence, saturation advertising, direct mail campaigns, reference group appeals, and celebrity testimonials.[85] He imbued his brand with such meaning that people would often buy two sets of the same pottery: one for use and one as a collectible.

People coveted Wedgwood products and the company endeavored to make them available to all without sacrificing quality. Knowing how pricing impacts a brand's image, Josiah Wedgwood wrote in 1772, "Low prices must beget low quality in the manufacture, which will beget contempt, which will beget neglect & disuse, and there is an end of the trade."[86] Wedgwood knew that a brand's relationship with consumers was as fragile as the pottery the company produced.

Wedgwood enticed buyers by educating them on the finer things in life. The showrooms featured elegant, large-scale displays with products that were beautifully arranged on tables that mimicked settings for dinners and teas. The company made it easy for customers to envision the china and pottery in their home.

The company stunned competitors and consumers alike—250 years ago—by offering free shipping anywhere in England, replacing damaged merchandise, and providing a money-back guarantee.[87] All of these interactions built a relationship of trust with his customers. The innovations, quality, and consistency have paid off for more than two centuries, given the iconic nature of the Wedgwood brand.

WHERE'S THE TRUST?

Gary Singer is a partner and the Chief Marketing Officer at global consulting firm A.T. Kearney. Gary discussed with me the basis of the relationship between brand and consumer. "Brands are in the eyes of the receiver, not the sender. A common misbelief about marketing is that the brand owner controls the brand. In fact, it is the exact opposite—the brand user creates and controls the brand. Marketing creates a relationship between the two that is meaningful to both."

Gary explained: "Simply stated, the relationship between company and consumer is a contract. As the brand owner I give you something that you value, and in return you give me your loyalty, your enthusiasm, your word of mouth, and hopefully, your ongoing usage. I consider *marketing* and *relationships* to be synonyms for each other."

In 2016, my company released a report about the way consumers purchase wine. We discovered that 76 percent of consumers have no idea what type or brand of wine they will purchase before entering the store. More than two-thirds make their choice based on the label. Most interesting was how intimidating wine buying is for many people. One respondent admitted, "Sometimes it feels like I am shopping for pornography. I am afraid to ask anyone for help and just want to get out of the store as quickly as possible."

After the report's release, I received a call from a brand manager at a leading winery. His winery's marketing efforts for their individual brands were tired and sales were slipping. The brand manager had presented the report's findings as a call to action for the winery to recapture market share by acting on the consumer insights.

The brand manager showed me his company's marketing plan and I was startled by its assumptions. Most of the content masqueraded as intimate knowledge of the customer.

Technology, speed, and the quest for growth have built an impersonal wedge between brand and consumer. The result is that many companies operate with inaccurate knowledge and do not have the best interests of consumers in mind. That is no way to build a relationship. This was the case with the winery. They had no idea what customers were basing purchase decisions on because they did not know their customers.

The chief building block of a fulfilling a longstanding relationship is trust. Marketers and brands ignore that fact at their peril. Nielsen's *Global Trust in Advertising* survey asks 28,000 consumers in 56 countries what forms of advertising they most trust. In the 2015 report, overwhelmingly, "recommendations from people I know" was chosen as number one. Meanwhile, trust in television, radio, newspaper, and magazine advertising has been steadily declining.

Relationships are more important than ever right now. And trust is the glue that makes any relationship work. It is easy to destroy trust through some sort of bad behavior, especially with millennials. This group is very aware of how brands and CEOs behave.

An example is the Barilla brand controversy. This 150-year-old pasta, sauce, and bread company made headlines in 2013. The CEO, Guido Barilla, said he favored "traditional" families and wouldn't use same-sex couples in advertising.[88] Those comments initiated a backlash and boycott that almost destroyed the brand overnight. Sales plummeted. The event changed the relationship between the brand and consumers. Trust was lost.

Brands will always get themselves into trouble, but they need to be honest. When trouble happens, companies should make a genuine apology and make tangible changes in practice.

Guido Barilla apologized for his statement twice. He commented on Facebook that he has "always respected every person I've met, including gays and their families, without any distinctions" and "never discriminated against anyone." The company created a diversity and inclusion board, launched a training program for employees and contributed to LGBT causes. Within a year the company scored a top rating on the Human Rights Campaign's list of employers who are LGBT-friendly.[89]

Consumers around the world are increasingly behaving the same way as our ancestors did. We are paying less attention to mass communications. Instead we are leaning on the fence chatting to our neighbors about their new car. We ask friends what golf clubs send the ball farther and what yoga studio has the best instructors. Our ears perk up when we hear about a deal a friend received on a barbecue grill. This extends to the online world where peer reviews help us select restaurants, books, cell phones, and everything else available for sale on the Internet. These reviews are now more compelling than a banner ad, coupon, or contest.

Seeking advice from other customers helps sort through the dizzying array of choices while proclaiming our allegiances and interests. "Word-of-mouth" advertising gives consumers added confidence to try a particular brand.

HOW CAN WE HELP?

Being intrusive has been a problem for marketing for over a century. Consider this from an editorial in the *London Times* in 1886: "The incessant witless repetition of advertisers' moron-fodder has become so much a part of life that, if we are not careful, we forget to be insulted by it."[90]

Marketing blogger Seth Godin writes, "Interruption Marketing is the enemy of anyone trying to save time. By constantly interrupting what we are doing at any given moment, the marketer who interrupts us not only tends to fail at selling his product, but wastes our most coveted commodity, time. In the long run, therefore, Interruption Marketing is doomed as a mass marketing tool. The cost to the consumer is just too high."[91]

Marketers are learning that the way to be effective is to be the opposite of intrusive. Making marketing a natural fit is the secret to getting people talking about and recommending your brand.

The Ford Motor Company has nurtured connections with consumers for over a century. Now the company plans to create different and deeper relationships by reaching "the next level in mobility, connectivity, and analytics" through its smartphone app, FordPass, that debuted in early 2016.[92]

FordPass claims to be "A Smarter Way to Move." Its website describes what is coming: "We are going to change how the world moves to make people's lives easier. Ford is taking steps big and small to bring you solutions that put you in control of the journey, giving you the power to experience your world more freely than ever before." This is a very big idea for a traditional car company.

The FordPass app is available for free to anyone, not just Ford car owners. FordPay is a virtual wallet that allows people to find and pay for parking. FordPay also works at participating fast food outlets. The company has also rolled out FordGuides, which is basically a free OnStar service. Drivers touch a button and speak live to personal mobility assistants called FordGuides who offer help finding routes and booking parking in advance.

FlightCar may be the most interesting part of Ford's new direction. It helps you share or borrow a vehicle when you travel. The goal of FlightCar is to optimize ride sharing, car sharing, and multi-modal transportation. Its goal is to get you from door to door in the most effective way possible.

Some functions are aimed at Ford owners. The app connects car owners with dealers to schedule maintenance and service appointments. Ford owners can add features like remote starting, locking and unlocking, checking fuel and oil levels and tire pressure. It also helps them locate their vehicles. FordPass is also building a loyalty program so users gain perks from affinity partners such as Spotify, BP, McDonald's, and 7-Eleven.

Not all of this will be virtual. The company plans new retail storefronts in urban areas called FordHubs. These are not traditional dealerships. The first stores are slated for New York (now open), San Francisco, London, and Shanghai. The company is serious about making this program work globally in the long term. According to the company website, FordHubs are, "where consumers will be able to explore Ford's latest innovations, learn about the company's mobility services and experience exclusive events."

At the launch of FordPass, president and CEO Mark Fields said, "From a customer standpoint, great experiences lead to long-term relationships. From a business standpoint, FordPass will drive greater loyalty, bring new consumers, and accelerate Ford in becoming a serious player in mobility services."[93] This puts Ford in a constant relationship with customers and prospects.

This is a campaign with grand ambitions. Ford is hopeful that FordPass will "do for car owners what iTunes did for music fans."[94] The entire initiative came from a small working group within the company that studied brands that have made relationship building their core difference. They looked at Apple, Disney, and Nike for inspiration and ideas. Everything they considered was researched and tested in detail by teams of anthropologists, sociologists, and digital experts.[95]

Why make such a move now? This new initiative is a response to a troubling trend for all auto manufacturers. Consumers are increasingly moving to urban centers and giving up car ownership. Ford sees its future in a broader definition of mobility. FordPass intends to provide a comprehensively connected consumer experience for owners and attract future buyers to the brand by meeting the gamut of their transportation needs.

It's been called "the beginning of the end of car ownership."[96] That transition is not something Ford is banking on, but it will certainly upend the traditional business model of a car company. Writer Nick Jaynes notes this is a "brand new position: becoming the helpful, insightful brand that helps you get where you want to go, whether it's behind the wheel of a Ford or on public transport."[97]

The FordPass marketing strategy is to build relationships. Ford is going beyond its traditional customer base, looking to stay in constant contact with consumers, and providing a range of valuable free services. The FordPass will change relationships, but no one can predict how or if it will sell more cars or replace those sales with a new revenue model. Who knows? Perhaps Ford Motor Company will be renamed "Ford Mobility Company"!

WOMEN DRINK BEER, TOO

Relationships are changing in other product categories too. I always puzzled over the lack of effort by beer companies to attract female consumers. Historically, beer marketing either objectified women or disregarded them altogether.[98] Beer marketers were hyper-focused on young males for decades. That is why we ended up with slews of pool party and sports-themed beer marketing.

A combination of societal and economic factors appears to be changing this male dominance. The craft beer category has nearly tripled in volume since 2010. Meanwhile, mainstream beer has lost ten percentage points of its volume share to wine and spirits since 2002. It is estimated that women now consume thirty percent of all craft beer and twenty-five percent of the entire beer category.[99]

Women are drinking beer and the beer companies are changing their marketing. Britt Dougherty, MillerCoors' Senior Director of Marketing Insights, said more gender-friendly marketing could increase sales five million to nine million additional barrels over the next five years.[100]

Coors Light developed a campaign called "Climb On" that was lauded for its efforts to include women in non-objectifying ways. The brand honored its roots with photos of climbers on mountain peaks. It included images of women scaling walls, running races, and white-water rafting. Dougherty is teaching her colleagues at MillerCoors "to never think about beer drinkers as consumers, or even 'targets,'" to help the brewer create "an emotional connection with the brand."[101] That connection helps build trust and maintain the relationship.

Bud Light's 2016 Super Bowl commercial featured comedians Amy Schumer and Seth Rogen in a political-themed ad called "Raise One to Right Now." One could hardly call it refined, as it was laced with sexual innuendo. All it did was establish parity between the genders with juvenile content. Still, it was a significant improvement over Bud Light's "Up for Whatever" campaign, from the previous year. That ad had used the tagline, "The perfect beer for removing 'no' from your vocabulary for the night," which people saw as an endorsement of date rape. The company apologized and stopped using the slogan.[102]

Heineken is trying an entirely different approach. It is appealing to moderate drinkers with ads that suggest modern women will be more attracted to men who drink less. One commercial featured women singing the Bonnie Tyler song "I Need a Hero" as they walk away from inebriated men.[103] This type of marketing is among the more interesting strategies to establish relationships with women.

Like the relationships in our personal lives, the relationship between brand and consumer takes work. Relationships are rewarding, dynamic, and fragile. It takes years to build trust and equity that can be eroded or destroyed in a moment. The most successful marketers obsess over building mutually beneficial relationships, and they know that relationship building is never finished.

CHAPTER 5

MARKETING CREATES COMMUNITY

"Community is much more than belonging to something;
it's about doing something together that makes belonging matter."[104]

BRIAN SOLIS, PRINCIPAL, ALTIMETER GROUP

Some brands encourage customers to band together into communities. Energy drink Red Bull and action camera maker GoPro are both powered by communities that provide passionate support to the brands.

Red Bull started as an energy drink company and built a community around the brand by leveraging sponsorship and events, word-of-mouth, merchandise, and social media. GoPro entered a crowded market and could have ended up just another camera company. Instead, it asked customers to "Be a Hero" and named its camera series "HERO." The company uses both web and social channels to empower and engage its community to drive brand interactions. It has developed a program of brand ambassadors and built showcases for fans to create content and share their GoPro experiences.

Both companies leverage the power of community, which psychologist Rollo May describes as follows: "Communication leads to community, that is, to understanding, intimacy and mutual valuing."[105]

Susan Fournier is a professor at Boston University, and Lara Lee spent fourteen years as vice president of enthusiast services at Harley-Davidson. In a 2009 article in the *Harvard Business Review*, they talked about the concept of building brand communities. "Often, people are more interested in the social links that come from brand affiliations than they are in the brands themselves. They join communities to build new relationships." As examples, the authors cite Facebook, country clubs, and churches, as well as "third place" brands like Gold's Gym and Starbucks that provide physical locations outside of work and home to foster interaction.[106]

In a subtle but powerful distinction, Fournier and Lee point out that brand preference "is the reward for meeting people's needs for community, not the impetus for the community to form."[107] In other words, people prefer a brand that supports an organically formed community that already exists, not a brand that manufactures a community.

Let's look at an example from the mid-twentieth century that illustrates the concept of brand community. We're at a suburban American neighborhood in 1954 where, in one home, a woman is preparing to host a Tupperware party.

It is two hours before the guests are to arrive and the hostess is nervous. She has repeatedly rearranged the living room furniture. Chairs are set up to create a theater atmosphere. The hostess is an enterprising entrepreneur who is taking a risk. Will this event be a success? It had better be, she thinks, since she has tapped her social network to fill the chairs. Her nervousness is understandable, considering she is putting her reputation on the line and breaking new ground.

At the appointed time, the invited guests arrive. Pleasantries are exchanged. Conversations do not go much beyond the weather and the innocent antics of children. Everyone compliments the hostess on her home while noting the living room's arrangement. Refreshments are served and the women begin to claim available seats. The hostess takes the stage by positioning herself in front of the guests. Carefully balancing their coffee cups, the ladies in attendance have no idea of the impact this gathering and so many like them will have on marketing and sales, women in business, and popular culture.

The man for whom Tupperware is named is not well-known. Earl Tupper got his start as a child selling farm produce door to door. The young Earl was more interested in inventing than selling. Tupper remained fascinated his whole life with design and how products solved everyday problems. He was a tinkerer who believed mistakes were part of the process of discovery. Tupper developed hundreds of new products, but only one really took off.[108]

That 1948 creation was originally called the "Wonder Bowl." The bowl laid claim to the name for several reasons. Its translucent polyethylene was molded specifically to store food. The patented "Tupper Seal," inspired by paint can lids, was a new feature. It stored food in an airtight and leak-free environment.[109] Liquid-filled Wonder Bowls were thrown across rooms to demonstrate how well they worked.[110]

You might assume Tupperware was an immediate success— that it quickly replaced glass, porcelain, and crystal. That is not true. Like many products today, Tupperware became known over time because of trend experts and style influencers. The first advocates of the plastic bowls were writers for leading magazines who highlighted its ease of use, functionality, and engaging design.

House Beautiful published an article entitled "Fine Art for 39 Cents." The author called the bowls "as good as a piece of sculpture."[111] One paragraph is effusive: "If you have never touched polyethylene, we need to tell you that it has the appearance of great fragility and delicacy—yet has great strength. It has the fingering qualities of jade, but at the same time reminds you of alabaster and mother of pearl. Held up to the light, it becomes opalescent and translucent and has an interesting, new ability to transfer light. So these bowls look like art objects—even before you know what they do."[112] In 1956 the Museum of Modern Art inducted Tupperware into its permanent collection.[113] This choice to artistically validate Tupperware's aesthetics was made with very little time passage for historic appraisal.

News stories and art world acceptance were fine, but the company needed sales. At the start, Tupperware was sold in hardware and department stores but the products failed to attract buyers. A flagship store on Fifth Avenue in New York City was more vanity than strategy and was shut down.

Tupperware would have an entirely different history if not for a woman named Brownie Wise. A divorcee with children and no formal education, Wise overcame many obstacles with quick wit, energy, and charm. She began her career selling Stanley home products through what is now called the party-planning system. She used that sales technique to dramatically increase sales for Tupperware.[114]

Wise adored Tupperware but realized it needed to be demonstrated to convince buyers. She began selling both Stanley and Tupperware products at the same party events but soon dropped Stanley. Wowed by her results, Tupper offered Wise a job. The two formed Tupper Home Parties in 1951 with Wise as president. Her first decision was to remove Tupperware from retail stores. From that point on, the party plan system became the company's exclusive method of marketing and selling.[115]

Party plan marketing leverages socializing and a promise that everyone in the process benefits. The promise is straightforward:

homemakers invite groups of friends to their homes for a unique product demonstration and light refreshments. The hostess in turn receives a gift of choice from the brand and takes orders from attendees.

Wise recognized that products sell better when recommended by friends and family. As noted in the "Tupperware!" episode of the PBS *American Experience* series, "Many fledgling Tupperware dealers found a willing and sympathetic first hostess in a close friend or a family member. It was these connections with female friends and relatives that usually got a Tupperware dealer's new business off the ground." Party plan marketing works because guests have a personal connection to the hostess or host.

Once hired, Wise wasted no time. She recruited and trained thousands of eager women as Tupperware representatives. By 1954, there were 20,000 members in the sales network.[116] The Tupperware Corporation soon moved to Florida where Wise created a theme park-like headquarters designed to impress. The sprawling complex held offices, party labs, an auditorium, and impressive grounds.

Tupperware parties provided women with a flexible means of working from home while generating income. They offered a form of independence and pride not previously enjoyed, though critics later accused the process of further domesticating women. Wise saw her efforts as a crusade to unshackle women from the kitchen even if that meant selling kitchen products.[117] In essence, she was creating two communities: one that sold, and one that gathered to buy. Tupperware was not a product. It was two cultures and communities that overlapped.

Tupperware is going strong. As of 1999, "A Tupperware party takes place somewhere in the world every two point five seconds, and an estimated 90 percent of American homes own at least one piece of Tupperware."[118] According to its 2016 annual report,

Tupperware Brands had a global sales force of 2.7 million in almost 100 countries in 2016, as well as sales revenues of $2.5 billion.

In the midst of runaway success, Wise and Tupper had a falling out and parted company in 1958. Tupper could not tolerate her lavish spending. In 1954, she became the first woman to appear on the cover of *Business Week*.[119] And Wise continues to attract attention. Bob Kealing's 2016 book, *Life of the Party: The Remarkable Story of How Brownie Wise Built, and Lost, a Tupperware Party Empire*, is being developed into a movie starring Sandra Bullock.[120]

Tupperware parties took advantage of the fact that marketing is a social activity. Wise observed how housewives interacted and how they shopped. Women swapped ideas and exchanged news of sales and specials. These activities reflect the need to share, connect, and affirm one's own choices. Tupperware offered more than a sealable plastic bowl: it leveraged our need to connect and congregate with like-minded people.

I experienced party plan marketing firsthand when my step-daughter announced she was having a Stella & Dot jewelry trunk show at our house. She heard about it from a friend and contacted the company. It fell largely on my wife to pull off the event and ensure there were enough guests to make a go of it.

Instead of vacating the house, I created a role for myself. As the official "pourer of wine," I lubricated the wheels of commerce. This was arguably an unfair factor for guests who may have already felt compelled to buy. Overall, I was impressed with the event. The description of the jewelry including background on the designs, materials used, and production process were interesting. Sales were strong. The Stella & Dot representative was pleased, and my wife received a gift and discount on purchases for hosting.

Different products are sold this way but remain targeted towards women. I think it would be smart to build communities of both genders. Wine and cooking would make for a fun party-plan evening. Male-only events are in short supply but could work. Golf, fishing, and barbecuing, though stereotypical activities, stand a good chance of succeeding. Imagine attending a barbecue evening with equipment and accessories that included actual cooking. Personally, I would attend one based around a scotch whiskey tasting, and you could not keep me away from a barbecue and scotch combination. I would become the president of that community.

Call it what you want: social retailing, multi-level marketing, or party planning, this type of marketing leverages your own network of generally like-minded individuals. Companies look for the quickest way to get to a sale. Your peer group has already congregated, established trust, and expressed shared interests. As long as the offer is above-board and mutually beneficial, why not leverage this channel that is predicated on our desire to connect and form communities? Let me know if you want an invite to the next scotch and barbecue.

BELONGING CREATES A SENSE OF BELONGING

What makes a community? What brings people together? Social psychologists David W. McMillan and David M. Chavis formed the most widely accepted understanding of how communities work and are credited with the term "a sense of community."[121] Communities give members a feeling of belonging among people with similar interests. A community provides safety, creates trust, and affirms our decisions. Members feel special and have pride in association. A community can be as diverse as fans of a sporting team or loyal members of a yoga studio or people who drive a Jeep Wrangler.

I am a member of the latter community. The only requirement of entry is Wrangler ownership. When I bought one, I was told by the salesperson to expect the "Jeep wave" from fellow Wrangler owners. What is the "Jeep wave"?

"An honor bestowed upon those drivers with the superior intelligence, taste, class, and discomfort tolerance to own the ultimate vehicle—the Jeep. Generally consists of vigorous side-to-side motion of one or both hands, but may be modified to suit circumstances and locally accepted etiquette."[122]

No one knows when or why this got started. One theory suggests it began during World War II when Jeeps were the workhorses of the American military. Jeep drivers would wave to fellow soldiers and, of course, salute superior officers. The wave signified a "sign of camaraderie and respect between courageous souls in dark and dangerous times."[123] Some believe it began after hostilities ended and the troops had come home. Former soldiers loved the Jeep vehicle and bought it for domestic use. That meant if you came across another Jeep, it was probably driven by a veteran. The wave was a former soldier's way of saluting.[124]

I remember smiling at the salesperson and discounting the story as part of the sales process. I was wrong. The moment I left the lot, other Jeep Wrangler owners were giving me the wave. I reciprocated as an acknowledgment of belonging to the club. I am now disappointed if I do not get the wave from a fellow member. I've read some therapy on this subject: "So next time you see a Jeep, give a wave and if you don't get one in return, don't be offended, just consider it a wave for the 'One and Only Jeep' and what it represents, our freedom and the brave souls who fought for it."[125]

As you would expect, Jeep is capitalizing on the wave phenomena. It has created an entire program around it, called "Jeep Wave": "The thrill of owning a Jeep Brand vehicle now extends beyond the road or trail with the Jeep Wave program. This exciting program rewards owners of select Jeep Brand models with a variety of exclusive benefits – like a dedicated number to call when you have questions, maintenance services and more."[126] The goal is to have Jeep owners waving with joy.

Jeep is not the only transportation company channeling the benefits of collective engagement. I sat down with Chris Brull, vice president of marketing at Kawasaki Motors USA, and talked community. Kawasaki is known for its motorcycles but it also manufactures bullet trains, tunneling equipment, rocket ships, gas turbines, and more. Our discussion focused on the company's power sports products. Chris told me the power sports division did some soul-searching during the recession a few years back.

According to Chris, Kawasaki viewed the downturn in business as an "opportunity to go out and reposition the brand. We talked to thousands of our customers, former executives, people back at the factory, designers, current owners, intenders (note: 'intenders' are people who are intending to buy, but haven't yet and could change their minds). We met with people and they vociferously told us 'Kawasaki is the intelligent rebel.'"

Chris asked himself, "What does that mean? I can't market 'Kawasaki: the Intelligent Rebel.'" He learned that people saw Kawasaki as a brand that's not for everyone. Chris explained, "We're about going faster, further, fiercer than everyone else. We are addicted to innovation, thrill seeking, and thrill achieving; no other brand actually claims that. And not everyone wants to be part of it."

Kawasaki's research included the competition. "Honda is seen as the 'conservative aristocrat.' Yamaha is the 'willful engineer' but is devoid of deep personality. Suzuki is the 'category challenger,' which means copycat, not only in products, but also in the way they market. The 'intelligent rebel' has swagger. It is similar to the Harley-Davidson brand personality, but Harley is about being an outlaw. Harley is very intimidating. Big bikes, big people. With us, a rebel is someone doing something different but is still inclusionary. We're like, 'Hey! Come on in! No problem! If we're not for you, it's all good! That's fine!' There's a very big inclusionary feeling with the Kawasaki community."

People who exemplify this notion of 'intelligent rebel' are basketball coach Phil Jackson, innovator Steve Jobs, and even the fictional Captain Kirk, said Chris. "Each one of those personalities was inspiring. They went their own way and it worked." Chris said he believes Kawasaki enjoys a unique community. "Since 1972, our tagline has been 'Let the Good Times Roll.' No matter what you ride, it's for good times. Our community loves to get out, have that wind in the face, dirt in the face, sand in the face, and have a good time."

These communities have to be real. "People can spot a fake," said Chris. "So they've asked us to be 'True to the Core.' It's a movement. It's not to be confused with 'Intelligent Rebel,' which is the brand positioning, and the tagline 'good times.' With this 'True to the Core' mantra, our community is telling us to be honest, real, authentic. Core means the core ride, but it also means who I am as a person, and why I ride. People say, 'Kawi gets me.' That's very powerful when you're motivating a community."

When communities are real and fulfill the needs of members, they provide validation of membership. Brands have always been like private member clubs. They give the impression of exclusivity but invite everyone to join. Kawasaki has an inclusionary approach but the brand is not for everyone. No brand is for *everyone*.

I AM YOU, YOU ARE ME

People within communities need and want to share. Sharing our life's experiences helps define who we are and helps validate and adjust our decisions. This explains why social media has become so influential. Social media is mostly a validating medium. If we get a "like," share, or retweet, we feel we are on the right track.

Our desire to develop and belong to communities has existed for millennia. Now we have access to the writings—or rather, wall inscriptions—of the community of everyday citizens during the Roman Empire. The *Corpus Inscriptionum Latinarum* is a database of more than 180,000 Roman inscriptions from plaster walls of buildings, tombstones, and city walls. This repository is a capture of Roman society's graffiti.

It is surprising to learn that this orderly republic was so defaced. The database is "an astonishing trove of pop culture—advertisements, gambling forms, official proclamations, birth announcements, magical spells, declarations of love, dedications to gods, obituaries, playbills, complaints, and epigrams."[127]

The collection "offers scholars a remarkable picture of every-day life: the tumult of the teeming streets in Rome, the clamor of commerce in the provinces, and the hopes and dreams of thousands of ordinary Romans—innkeepers, ointment sellers, pastrycooks, prostitutes, weavers, and wine sellers. The world revealed is at once tantalizingly, achingly familiar, yet strangely alien, a society that both closely parallels our own in its heedless pursuit of pleasure."[128]

Speaking of pleasure, the *Corpus* holds many writings on wine. The favored brand of white wine, Falernian, could be as old as 160 years. These aged vintages were reserved for the emperor and the ruling class, but, "Roman oenophiles could purchase younger vintages of Falernian, and they clearly delighted in bragging of its expense." [129]

Centuries before disgruntled consumers shared bad experiences on Yelp, one Roman citizen took exception to his treatment at a pub. He left this message on its wall: "May cheating like this trip you up, bartender. You sell water and yourself drink undiluted wine."[130] Not only did he call the man a crook, he implied that the bartender was a barbarian. Ouch.

This wall writing is not unlike the original Facebook wall, which in 2011 was replaced by the timeline. Facebook is a modern day *Corpus* collecting the likes, shares, and opinions of our society. Decades and centuries from now, historians and sociologists may analyze our society's content on Facebook to understand people and the communities they belonged to.

Romans emphasized family, lived in a defined neighborhood, favored one bathhouse over another, cheered for specific gladiators, and patronized their preferred wine outlet. An individual lived in several communities simultaneously.

The same thing happens today. Curiously, our many different memberships communicate who we are as individuals. Every one of us is a complex collective made up of different interests, activities, and associations.

No society or community is completely homogeneous. There are different divisions, cliques, teams, and tribes even when there is a common language, ethnicity, and culture. Back to the Jeep wave (the hand gesture, not the marketing program). It applies *only* to Wrangler owners, not other Jeep vehicles. So if you own a Patriot,

Renegade, Compass, Cherokee, or Grand Cherokee, do not expect a wave.

COMMUNITIES DEFINE US

A community is a group of people who share a particular characteristic. Marketers strive to make brands match that common characteristic. Throughout its 65-year history, Lego has stayed true to its mission of inspiring children to think creatively.[131] There is much lore about this brand. Lego fans know that every brick has a number that identifies the mold it came from.[132] Pieces as far back as 1958 will click into today's product.[133] A Danish mathematician discovered that the originally patented six Lego bricks can be combined to produce over nine hundred million different configurations.[134]

More of these facts came to light in *Beyond the Brick: A LEGO Brickumentary*. The film celebrates all things Lego, including the community of fans both young and old, the Brick Conventions, theme parks, and pop-culture omnipresence. The television show *The Simpsons* commemorated its 550th episode by presenting the characters in Lego brick form. A review of *The Lego Movie*, which grossed over $500 million, said, "*The Lego Movie* is a 3-D animated film that connects."[135] Connecting is exactly what Lego does.

But the ride has not always been smooth. During a boom period in the late 1990s, Lego aggressively increased the number of bricks. The company invested in unique and customized pieces with more bells and whistles. Lego sets became too complex. Production costs soared and soon sales fell. Even the most faithful of the Lego community were turned off.[136]

By 2003 Lego was almost bankrupt. It took years and a more rigorous design process to bring down the number of bricks. Lego learned the hard way that products are one-dimensional (so to speak), but the brand has many layers, tenets, and beliefs.

Lego has since rebuilt trust, and the community is stronger. More than 5,000 tickets were purchased for the BrickCan in Vancouver, Canada in 2016. This event and thousands like it, held every year and organized by Lego fans all around the world, give Lego fans the opportunity to get together to discuss the love of the bricks and share unique designs.[137]

Twins Brandon and Taylor Walker, age 21, attended BrickCan. Brandon showed off a life-sized version of Thor's magical hammer he made out of 1,500 Lego bricks. Taylor created Captain America's shield. It was designed digitally, took two weeks to complete, and required 3,500 pieces. Unlike some enthusiasts who build elaborate statues only to knock them down, the Walker brothers keep their creations intact and bring them to conventions.[138]

Lego is not a cheap proposition. Sets cost hundreds of dollars. Robin Sather, chairman of the BrickCan Foundation, says that hardcore Lego community members spend thousands of dollars a year. Sather explains the fascination: "I think for me it's the safe creativity. The things you can make with Lego is infinite, but there are only certain ways Lego can go together. It's not intimidating. They just go together. A blank canvas or a lump of clay, well that's a little more intimidating."[139]

In 2013, Lego overtook Hasbro to become the world's second-largest toymaker.[140] The number one toy company, Mattel, bought the Canadian maker of Mega Bloks to try to fend off Lego's challenge.[141]

The appeal of Lego spans generations. The bricks give creative freedom to children, and the brand appeals to the nostalgia of a segment of adults who still enjoy building and creating with tactile objects. Children who have never met can instantly bond over Lego. Adults choose to spend their vacations at Lego fan events. One thing's for sure: the toy builds communities.

TRIBAL BRANDFARE

How we group ourselves and what we support is mostly a mystery, yet marketers have attempted to develop a framework for understanding this social complexity. We seek some form of kinship, value reciprocal exchanges, and benefit from social interaction and communication. The new term from sociologists and consumer behaviorists is "brand tribes."[142]

These tribes are groups of people linked around a brand by a shared belief.[143] Tribe members are not simply consumers, they are believers and promoters. These brand tribes are capable of collective action, especially in the age of social media.[144]

Coca-Cola and Pepsi have recognized the importance of brand tribes and like most global brands, are trying to find a way to attract and create loyal collectives. Coca-Cola launched its "Share a Coke" campaign in 2014. Coke tags bottles with hundreds of different names. Consumers post pictures of themselves after searching through stores to find their names and the names of friends and family on bottles. Said Coca-Cola executive Jennifer Healan, "Share a Coke gave the brand a new way to do something we've done for almost 129 years: connect people."[145] The campaign continues in 2018.

The 2016 "Say It With Pepsi" campaign was rolled out in over 100 countries. Pepsi created hundreds of emoji designs that had both global appeal and were tailored to local markets. Pepsi drinkers posted images to social media paired with unique hashtags. The emojis included one taking a selfie, another snorkeling, one waving a flag, and another gushing tears of joy. In an interview in *USA Today* about Pepsi's campaign, I suggested that the fact that emojis have become a shared language is the reason why a brand like Pepsi can make use of them to help build their brand tribes.[146]

Emojis are modern-day pictograms that have been used throughout the ages. Pictures representing words were used in ancient Sumeria, Egypt, and China. Sumerians invented them around 3000 BC as wedge-shaped icons representing sounds, ideas, and things.[147] Later, Phoenician traders took this form of communication to Greece, where the locals turned it into a 22-character alphabet. Today, marketing agencies create systems of pictograms that transcend language, culture, and custom. Pictograms, emojis, and logos are attempts at a shared language to create new communities and cultures.

John Naisbitt, author of *Megatrends*, has observed, "The more universal we become the more tribal we act."[148] Modern tribalism has us seeking out authentic, genuine, and trustworthy relationships and communities.

Small businesses create interesting communities. These enterprises are often labors of love. People start bike shops, restaurants, and yoga studios because they want to serve and work locally. Owners take great pride in what they are building, but the pressure to create a community is even greater given the rate of small business failure.

Collectively, small businesses are a significant force that has been professionally underserved and fractured. American Express recognized this and saw an opportunity to better serve this "tribe." Instead of sinking dollars into a traditional advertising campaign, American Express created an inspired marketing program geared specifically to small businesses.

To promote small business credit cards, the company created a forum for small business owners in 2007, American Express OPEN. The credit cards offered tailored buying power, customer service, rewards, expense management, and partner discounts.[149] Two other initiatives have cemented the community. The Open Forum website is an enormous repository of small business advice organized by subjects including planning for growth, managing money, getting customers, and building your team. Blogs, studies, and articles are researched, written, and shared specifically for this community. Small business owners swap and share their own experiences.

In 2010, American Express created Small Business Saturday, an annual one-day event.[150] It is positioned as a new shopping holiday held on the Saturday following American Thanksgiving. Small Business Saturday puts the focus on shopping at local small businesses rather than national retailers, big box stores, or online. In 2015, according to the American Express website, 73.9 million consumers spent $16.2 billion on the day, a fourteen percent increase over 2014. That year, even President Obama and his family participated, making purchases at a local bookstore and buying treats at a neighborhood ice cream shop in Washington, DC.[151]

The program has evolved with American Express leveraging and extending the power of community. It is one thing to have a day dedicated to patronizing small business, but what about the rest of the year? The program now has neighborhood champions who ensure that the message gets out year-round. These champions are themselves small business owners who rally other owners to coordinate local marketing efforts, much like an old-time marketplace.

American Express has created a trademark for this activity: "Shop Small." Merchants can download printable signage, email templates, social media templates, "Shop Small" logos, online ad space, and appear on the "Shop Small" map. Neighborhood champions organize parades, scavenger hunts, breakfasts, and award shows to bring continuous attention to local small business.[152] The entire program respects and leverages our tribal nature and our history.

In 2012, Gartner Research identified ten consumer trends that would have impact for the next ten years. One was the "renegotiation of consumer trust." The report said that consumers are "seeking new institutions, brands, and values to trust in. The collapse of confidence in traditional institutions following bank failures, government collapse, corruption, economic and civil unrest, and the disruption to previously accepted 'norms' (such as local communities and nuclear families) have sent consumers searching for new brands, values, and social organizations that they can trust. Brands that help their customers through hard times can build strong emotional and cognitive loyalty among consumers."[153]

It is no coincidence that tribalism has grown at the same time as the serious decline in trust of long-established institutions. People are seeking new, more intimate, and hopeful communities. It goes beyond simple membership. Community is about doing something *together* that matters. The goal is deep commitment through mutually beneficial support.

CHAPTER 6
MARKETING DELIVERS EXPERIENCES

"We see our customers as invited guests to a party, and we are the hosts. It's our job every day to make every important aspect of the customer experience a little bit better."[154]

JEFF BEZOS, FOUNDER AND CHIEF EXECUTIVE OFFICER, AMAZON

How sophisticated do you think marketing was in seventeenth-century London? Advertisements from that time reveal a society awash in a wide array of goods and services. These goods and services were advertised in the city's newspapers that were provided free in the 500 coffeehouses throughout the city. The population was nearing 500,000, which equates to one coffeehouse for every 1,000 residents. That number is even higher than present-day Seattle, the US city with the most coffee shops per resident (one coffee shop for every 2,200 people).

Free newspapers were available in old London coffeehouses, the equivalent of today's coffee shops offering Wi-Fi and phone charging stations. This was all part of marketing—to attract and retain customers by delivering a pleasurable experience.

One of the most famous coffeehouses in seventeenth-century London was Garraway's. It was grand, in a building with more than ten fireplaces and chimneys. Its prominent corner location and various entrances attracted impressive numbers of customers. Garraway's stayed in business for two hundred years before finally closing in 1866. All that remains of this historic gathering place is a plaque marking the original site and a woodcut panel on a door. The panel reads, "Garraway's Coffee House, a place of great commercial transaction and frequented by people of quality."[155]

The woodcut depicts a scene from the coffeehouse. It shows one gentleman with his nose firmly in a newspaper absorbing current affairs. Three other men are forever frozen in a lively debate. Garraway's and competing coffeehouses on the same street attracted patrons who would go on to form the London Stock Exchange. These regulars are the equivalent of today's entrepreneurs who make coffeehouses their offices.

The proprietor, Thomas Garraway, was the first retailer of tea in England. He marketed the beverage by stressing its medicinal benefits. Later he sold coffee to a well-heeled business crowd. The main floor of Garraway's was divided into small dining rooms while the top floor housed the coffeehouse. It was a place where the clientele debated the issues of the day or sat alone writing or reading.

Coffeehouses were known as "penny universities."[156] Politics, gossip, fashion, current events, and philosophy were explored. London coffeehouses were lively places. As described by Brian Cowan in his history of British coffeehouses, "The coffeehouse was a place for like-minded scholars to congregate, to read, as well as learn from and to debate with each other, but was emphatically not a university institution, and the discourse there was of a far different order than any university tutorial."[157]

Garraway's resembled a library with well-upholstered mahogany boxes for seating. Rows of blackboards held the menu. The din of conversation was much louder than modern coffeehouses. Patrons were given free copies of the *London Gazette*, the *Spectator*, the *Athenian Mercury*, and other publications. The advertisements in these newspapers show that this period was far from austere.

Older homes with character or new builds were found in the real estate listings. Once purchased, insurance companies were eager to help protect the investment. A household cistern could be acquired to avoid the city's notorious hygiene issues and poor water supply. If the house needed repairs, wainscoting artisans, re-roofing services, and stained-glass craftsmen were on call. Imported Italian marble for floors and "crushed cockle-shells to spread on garden walks" could spruce up the home's aesthetics.[158]

One advertisement suggests that every gentleman's den must have a terrestrial or astronomical globe. Crystal decanters were marketed as status symbols. Book collections could be bought to communicate wealth and intellect. Guitar and singing lessons were offered. Men could pamper themselves with a shave and a massage while women could have excess hair and freckles removed. Real tortoise-shell eyeglass frames, gilded birdcages, and guided getaways to Holland were spoken about in eloquent and compelling phrases.[159]

While customers drank coffee, read, and debated, Thomas Garraway obsessed over their experience. He constantly looked for ways to differentiate his coffeehouse. Modern coffeehouses are known for setting up co-branding arrangements with other businesses. But this strategy began centuries ago. Garraway's had an exclusive relationship with G. Nash's kidney remedy. Those experiencing kidney discomfort were compelled to visit Garraway's to buy the medicine. Lloyd's Coffeehouse sold a curious mix of brandy, wine, and financial securities. No doubt this combination led to more than a few poor investment decisions. White's Coffeehouse patrons placed bets on how long customers had to live. This activity birthed the life insurance industry.[160]

A floating coffeehouse, The Folly of the Thames, was moored in the river. It became a rowdy dance hall every evening. Lunt's was a combination coffeehouse and barbershop—not a bad concept to consider today.[161] Coffeehouses encouraged patrons to stick around and write, much the way Starbucks, Au Bon Pain, Costa Coffee, Pret a Manger, Lavazza, and thousands more do today. Adam Smith wrote a good deal of *The Wealth of Nations* in a coffeehouse.[162]

The number one lesson coffeehouses learned: do not rush a patron. Give customers time to enjoy their beverages and bang out a manuscript or have a debate. Welcoming and comfortable experiences ensured regulars spent more time and money and attracted new patronage. The story of these old London coffeehouses prove that marketing based on delivering a deliberate and great experience has been highly sophisticated for a very long time.

EXPERIENCES OVER POSSESSIONS

Psychological research has shown that experiences are more valued than possessions. A 2014 study even found that the anticipation of money spent on experiences provides more enduring happiness than anticipating the purchase of material goods.[163]

The perceived value of experiences challenges long accepted marketing theory. Marketers have thought that people use possessions to identify themselves. Our choice of car, phone, jeans, and sunglasses are supposed to tell the world who we are. But it is not the thing itself that is important; it's what the thing promises and represents.

Possessions deteriorate, become obsolete, or teeter towards irrelevance. We will never remember the features of our third-last smartphone but we will remember how it helped us and how it made us feel. It's the experience of the item, not the item itself, that we value more.

Thomas Garraway's coffeehouse offered an experience. Today Starbucks and so many other coffee shops offer a similar kind of experience. Marketers talk about experiences all the time, but few make a customer's experience consistently right and sufficiently different. Most businesses focus on components like customer service but cannot see the entirety of how people wish to be treated.

Howard Belk, co-CEO and chief creative officer at branding agency Siegal + Gale, talked with me about the value of the customer experience. Howard explained, "Experiences are a must. Before we take any solution to a client we ask, 'Is the answer we're giving a yesterday answer or is it a tomorrow answer?' That is a simple reminder to help our clients think ahead. Experiences are a tomorrow answer. You have to have them. When it comes to gifts, the most memorable gifts are experiences. Going to the movie, or even doing a hike. Those experiences bring more happiness than very posh hard gifts."

But how do you make a product like a pack of gum or widget an experience? Howard said, "There are different kinds of experiences. We make sure that they're clear, that they're innovative, that they're valuable, that they have utility, and the people can navigate them. We call the critical elements 'unheralded touch points' because they're not obvious but they make a difference."

Howard used this technique with a client, Allstate Insurance. "Allstate came to us for a very specific purpose. They were losing one million customers a month in their auto insurance business. Yet, at the same time, they were winning one million new customers a month. They had customer churn that was phenomenally expensive." Joe Tripodi, senior vice president and chief marketing officer at Allstate, hired Howard's firm after having his own bad personal experience with Allstate. Shortly after joining the company, Tripodi decided to sign up for Allstate's auto insurance. He went through the process and was declined!

Tripodi found the experience difficult and the result "curt, abrupt, and unpleasant." Howard's firm examined the experience and concluded it was "really sub-optimal, off-putting, confusing, and unclear. We found there were 57 different correspondence types between Allstate and an auto insurance customer. All of the correspondence was via form letters and online notices. The language was inconsistent, the headings and titles of the documents misleading, and there was no continuity between them."

The number of letters and e-mails was overwhelming, but the worst crime was they were not personalized. Said Howard, "There was no recognition of the most valuable customers. There are many, many Allstate customers whose whole family, from grandparents to grandchildren, are customers, and who insure multiple vehicles."

Howard's team found that although marketing was ultimately responsible for all of these touch points, the Allstate legal department had added legalese, jargon, and clauses throughout the various communications. Footnotes and references were longer than the core content. Howard said, "They were taking all the humanity out of it. And stuff kept getting added to the content of the correspondence over time."

Of the 57 types of correspondence, more than twenty provided the option of cancelling the insurance. By reducing and simplifying these touch points, there was a dramatic impact. Churn was reduced and the customer experience was improved. According to Howard, "Costs went down and retention went up."

PASS THE HEINZ

Henry Heinz knew how to make products an experience. He came along at a time when people had little variety in what they ate. In the mid-1800s, families recycled a handful of simple recipes handed down from generation to generation. The family meal had limited choice. People shopped in bulk, did not know where the food came from, and purchased products that offered no quality or sanitary guarantee. Food and the ritual of mealtime were certainly not the rich experiences they are today.

According to Heinz, "a wide market awaited the manufacturer of food products who set purity and quality above everything else in their preparation."[164] Heinz believed, "To do a common thing uncommonly well brings success."[165]

Henry Heinz's unwavering belief in individually packaged products propelled the company forward. As a marketer, he recognized that when consumers purchased in bulk, there was no opportunity to make a name for the product. Individual product packaging changed all that.

Heinz was confident that people would adjust their behavior if his company could change the experience. He organized a direct sales force that transferred knowledge to shopkeepers who, in turn, educated consumers. Shoppers were attracted to the promise of something new that was helpful and valuable. Heinz made meal education an experience, something akin to today's Apple in-store Genius Bars.

The company is well known for ketchup, but it started with horseradish. Heinz used his mother's recipe and followed it up with sweet pickles, India relish, mustard dressing, tomato soup, and tomato chutney. Consumers saw these as exotic options and convenient solutions. Heinz tomato ketchup debuted in 1876.

Henry Heinz was a stickler for detail and a talented showman who jumped on every opportunity to place his brands at shows and fairs so people could see, try, and buy them. This interaction offered both entertainment and education, creating memorable experiences. Tastings were a big part of the marketing because a product sampled tended to be a product sold. Heinz employees took questions and were seldom stumped.

Heinz made sure that everyone who visited his displays at shows and fairs went home with something. Giveaways included calendars, spoons, greeting cards, and recipe books. Heinz personally loved collecting souvenirs, so he correctly assumed that people would appreciate the items, which would also help increase brand awareness and loyalty.

Heinz was a master at promotion. He installed the first electric sign in Manhattan with a 1,200-bulb array stretching six stories high along the side of the famous Flatiron Building. The installation instantly became a New York City attraction when it was first lit in 1900. The cutting-edge technology spelled out two different messages at blinking intervals. Company records indicate the electricity cost $90 each night or approximately $2,500 in today's dollars.[166]

One of Heinz's most amazing investments in the Heinz brand experience was the Heinz Pier in Atlantic City. The 900-foot pier jutted out into the ocean and had an ornate pavilion at its end. At the pier, the company hosted attractions, tours, and seminars, in the style of a P. T. Barnum circus.[167] Everything at the pier centered on the innovative production of Heinz products and how they influenced the experiences of buying, cooking, and eating. Heinz Pier paved the way for today's Busch Gardens, Hershey Park, and the World of Coca-Cola.

The company maintained the pier for 46 years, from its

construction in 1898 to 1944. During that time, over fifty million people visited the pier, and no one walked away empty-handed. Each guest received a collectible pin in the shape and color of a pickle.[168]

The Heinz ketchup bottle's iconic shape is recognized globally, but it breaks one rule of packaging design. While it protects and preserves the ketchup, it takes a long time for the ketchup to hit the plate, unlike most containers that are designed to dispense their contents with ease and speed.

Heinz prides itself on maintaining a ".028 miles per hour speed of exit," and if the ketchup leaves at a faster rate, that ketchup is rejected for sale.[169] There is a tricky solution to speed up the flow: "To release ketchup faster from the glass bottle, apply a firm tap to the sweet spot on the neck of the bottle—the '57.'"[170]

Today, because of consumer demand for faster ketchup flow, nearly 75 percent of Heinz tomato ketchup is sold in squeezable plastic bottles.[171] This packaging eliminates clogging and increases the ketchup's flow velocity. Yet, many people prefer the familiarity and nostalgia of the glass bottle. Heinz sells over 650 million bottles of ketchup every year in more than 140 countries.[172]

Much to the dismay of environmentalists, Heinz also sells eleven billion single-serve packets of ketchup annually.[173] When the company learned from consumers that the old packets were messy, especially in the family car when eating drive-thru fast food, Heinz started its research on the single-serving ketchup experience. Heinz staffers watched consumers behind one-way glass, checking how people in 20 fake minivan interiors put ketchup on fries, burgers, and chicken nuggets.[174]

In 2010, after three years of research, Heinz released new Dip and Squeeze ketchup packets. These offer three times more ketchup and provide a strong visual clue for consumers as they mimic the shape of the original bottle. Heinz used consumer experience research to develop the new packet. Maintaining Heinz pier, minting fifty million pickle pins, researching how consumers put ketchup on their fast food in the car—these efforts all attest to Heinz's faith in the power and cost-effectiveness of creating experiences.

WE BUY WHAT WE DO

At Quebec's Mont Tremblant ski resort there are two merchants who do a good job of showing off their food products. One sells maple syrup with a twist. There are layers of crushed ice in a large barrel outside the shop's entrance. Six-inch long shallow grooves are made in the ice. For $2.50 you "buy" one of these little furrows and it is filled with warm maple syrup. You are given a Popsicle stick to roll up the syrup as it slowly hardens from contact with the ice. It makes for a lick-able, portable and natural treat, and you feel as if you have made it. This hands-on introduction prompts purchasers to enter the store and buy higher-priced, margin-rich items.

The other merchant sells fudge. The smell from the shop is enticing, but it's the cook in the storefront window who provides action and theater. It is fun to watch different flavors of fudge concocted on a large slab of granite. An over-sized wooden paddle pushes around the gooey mass until it is cooled and cut for sale. The performance invites entry, questions, and interaction. It is far more effective than a sign in the window.

Demonstrating uses of food has been a standard for marketplaces from the beginning of history. Built for the exchange of goods, marketplaces also facilitate the exchange of knowledge. Vendors sell while dispensing advice such as explaining how a tool works, how a food can be prepared, or what wine to serve with it. Each vendor shares his or her unique expertise with the public. I have a favorite fish smokehouse that I visit. The owner is a treasure trove of know-how. Every interaction is a pleasant education. I buy the fish, but I get more than food in the process.

On a family vacation in Spain in the early 1970s my mother insisted we visit the Lladro City of Porcelain. She was a collector and our home was well stocked with figurines. My mother's collection had grown to the point of roping off the living room like a museum display.

The factory tour followed a figurine from start to finish. Each artist explained his or her contribution to the process. The visit was entertaining and further cemented my mother's preference for Lladro. She left with two more figurines.

When Isaac Singer introduced his famous sewing machine, he recognized that an experience with the machine was critical to getting people comfortable with its capabilities and operation. Until this point people's homes did not contain complex equipment. The Singer sewing machine changed that. The company relied on door-to-door sales. The product was brought right into the home and the pitch focused on simplifying one's life. The company also rolled out "flashy showrooms where it could demonstrate how the machines work, and took machine demonstrations to county and state fairs."[175]

Good vendors are adept at recognizing and honoring loyal customers. They know the value of someone returning time and again, along with the impact of positive word-of-mouth from satisfied customers.

I recall getting an early morning haircut at a barbershop in my hometown of Winnipeg. It was located in an underground mall in the city's downtown business district. While I was having my hair cut, another gentleman entered. The well turned-out fellow wore a custom pinstripe suit with a fresh red rose in his lapel. He was impeccably groomed, and I wondered what he required in the way of barbering.

The owners of the shop greeted him with familiarity and whisked him to a waiting chair. He was treated to an old-time shave and the quickest hair trim I ever witnessed. After the man departed the barber explained that the fellow came in every morning for the same treatment. It was a daily ritual that included purchasing the rose at the neighboring florist. Both establishments made sure never to disappoint, given the frequency of the customer's patronage.

When marketers speak of experiences they are still mostly talking about creating awareness and providing a bit of entertainment in the process. People learn much better by doing, and they have greater affinity for a brand that involves them in interesting and meaningful ways.

British retailer Topshop has a mission to open up the world's top fashion shows to more and more people. Topshop provides to the public an experience once only known to models and insiders. In 2013 at London Fashion Week, Topshop invited more fashion fans to experience the excitement and exclusivity of a runway show than ever before.

Topshop had live HD micro-cameras built into the clothes of the models to show the perspective of actually walking the runway. Topshop's chief marketing officer Justin Cooke said, "This is the complete democratization of a fashion show. The idea is that no one has ever seen that moment when the girl walks down the catwalk. You never know what it feels like to be her, so the emotive side is really important to us—we want to really make that connection with people."[176]

That London fashion show was the most watched runway

show in history, with over four million people tuning in live. In subsequent years, the retailer has expanded on the idea of insider access. Topshop partnered with Twitter to identify live trends during fashion week events around the world.[177] People became active participants in the fashion process. The activity on Twitter provided Topshop with incredible insights for future fashion ideas while validating current merchandising. The emerging trends identified by those who participated were shown on digital billboards in real time.

Topshop also partnered with Facebook so viewers could customize items from the "Topshop Unique" range of clothing as they appeared on the catwalk and buy the clothes and accessories online.[178] In a few short years, Topshop turned consumers into models, style experts, designers, and merchandisers. They invited customers to have a look behind the scenes. These innovations have completely upended the notion of traditional retailing.

WHERE EXPERIENCE MEETS COMMUNITY

In the past few years I have been exposed to the Ironman phenomenon. These grueling contests have participants who swim 2.4 miles, bike 112 miles, and run a 26.2-mile marathon. My wife and I have volunteered as security, hospitality representatives, and bike course monitors.

The Ironman triathlon events take over the host community. The organizers build a circus-like center, which is the gathering point for athletes, family, and spectators. On a visit to one giant tent where Ironman clothing, gear, and souvenirs were sold, I was struck by the setting. A man on a loudspeaker extolled the virtues of all things Ironman with emotional fervor. The tent and the atmosphere conjured up images of a Southern Baptist revival sermon. All around were symbols supporting the Ironman belief system. It smacked of organized religion.

This was a very structured and immersive experience. Theology and creed were on display, ceremony and ritual undeniable, symbolism and code spoke loudly, and there was even myth and mysticism in the reverent tones paid to past competitors.

I wanted to be part of the experience without making a physical effort, so I stood patiently in line to purchase an Ironman hat. The extensive pop-up store featured an impulse purchase laneway. As I made my way towards the cashiers, I took in the racks of Ironman promotional items. On a peg protruding from a rack was a silver object, whose package read, "Ironman Official Merchandise Auto Emblem."

Before any organ music started I completed the purchase and made my getaway. My last realization was that the competition was held on a Sunday, cementing the religious comparisons.

The Ironman experience is amazing. But I wonder: What came first, the community or the experience? The two are inextricably linked and that makes the Ironman brand formidable but not immune to changing tastes. The Ironman organizers have recognized the need to incorporate a new generation into its competition.

At the beginning of each major Ironman event there used to be a fun run for the children of competitors. Now there are Ironkid competitions, where competitors ages one (presumably in strollers) to fifteen compete in a race. As the website states, "Each athlete receives a race bib, finisher shirt, medal, goodie bag, and the pride of calling themselves an IRONKID!"[179] This is a clear indoctrination to the experience and community to help ensure their ranks will never thin.

Another immersive experience visits my community. The

Wanderlust Festival is held throughout North America mostly at other ski resorts like Whistler, Stratton, and Squaw Valley. It has its own brand of devotees. Co-founder Jeff Krasno discovered and capitalized on the fact that festivals are all about community. Wanderlust combines live music with daily yoga classes, hiking, organic food and wine, and inspirational speakers such as Deepak Chopra, all set in the great outdoors.

I wandered about this event and recognized a similar but different zealotry from Ironman. Wanderlust has a belief system built on mindfulness, eating well, group exercise, and being environmentally conscious, all while supporting the local arts and culture of the host community. There is a commercial aspect to the experience but the marketing is subdued. Numerous vendors take part in the festival, from global brands like Lululemon to small health food companies. There is no hard sell because attendees have already bought in to the goals and structure of the community.

Ironman, Wanderlust, and obstacle course endurance events like Spartan and Tough Mudder are very popular. The competitions are sporadic events, but they are ongoing experiences that demand their followers practice the beliefs of the community throughout the year. Ironman, Tough Mudder, and Spartan work because people want to claim a unique accomplishment. Both challenge participants to dig deep physically and emotionally. Spartan declares "Spartan Race is more than a race; it's a way of life."[180]

I spoke with a Tough Mudder marketing manager and was surprised to learn that their customer base is extremely diverse, ranging in every possible way from age to socio-economic to fitness level to race and gender. Tough Mudder's website states, "every Monday after a Tough Mudder event weekend is an official Wear Your Headband to Work Day, aka Headband Monday."[181] Tough Mudder participants are urged to post photos of themselves wearing the coveted headband to Tough Mudder's Facebook page. The Tough Mudder experience promises belonging and achievement, a powerful proposition.

If experiences are now more valued than possessions, marketers can drive sales through hands-on and immersive experiences. Think of it this way: the brand is the host and the consumer is the guest. Show customers a good time and they will keep coming back and will probably bring a few friends along.

CHAPTER 7

MARKETING DEMANDS AUTHENTICITY

"Mass advertising can help build brands,
but authenticity is what makes them last."[182]

HOWARD SCHULTZ, CHAIRMAN EMERITUS, STARBUCKS

If I tell you I am funny, cool, or smart, will you believe me? Every business and brand claims to be something, but how do we know the claim is credible?

Authenticity tends to be an overused and misapplied word in marketing and business these days. Authenticity is not a strategy or tactic; it is an expression of why a customer should believe in you. It tells people what you believe in as a company.

Rick Maynard, senior manager of public relations at KFC, spoke about brand authenticity: "To us, being real means being honest, inclusive, boldly unapologetic, refreshingly to the point, insightful and occasionally, a little edgy. We steer clear of being artificial, judgmental, insecure, full of hot air, timid, or gimmicky. We try to celebrate our real fans, engage in real talk, and encourage real consumer-generated content. We prefer 'man on the street' images over staged food shots. That's what being authentic means to our brand. And the great thing about being real is it's also really *easy*. It's much more difficult to try to be something you're not."[183]

Being something you are not, making false or misleading claims, over-promising and under-delivering, are all authenticity killers. Public relations agency Cohn & Wolfe, in its 2014 Authentic Brands study, surveyed twelve thousand people in twelve markets across the world. The study revealed that 91 percent of customers value honest communication from companies and 63 percent prefer to patronize authentic brands over competitors.[184] This research shows that consumers are holding companies accountable to what they say and how they act.

Chris Hummel, CMO at United Rentals, shared an amusing story with me on the subject of authenticity. "When I lived in Singapore," said Chris, "there was an area you could visit that sold knockoff goods—purses, sunglasses, wallets, watches, and jewelry. One of the stands had a sign that read, 'Genuine Imitation.' What in the world does 'genuine imitation' mean? They were claiming to produce very high quality knockoffs! You had to admire the honesty. But that is why authenticity is more than honesty."

Authenticity goes deeper than telling the truth. It means sticking to your ideals and keeping relevant to what made you successful and different in the first place.

MMM...SMELLS GOOD!

Today's luxury goods industry is worth $250 billion annually. The brands that make up this market owe their success to the decision-making of a group of French perfume manufacturers in the late 1800s. That group defined what was "authentic" in their industry.

Perfume manufacture has a rich history. The world's oldest known varieties were found on Cyprus, the island that claims to be the birthplace of Aphrodite, the Greek goddess of love, lust, and beauty. In 2003, archeologists unearthed evidence of early perfumes and their trade that proved aromatic scents date back more than four thousand years. This discovery included the oldest perfume-making factory in the world. This three thousand square-foot facility was part of a large complex of buildings, the equivalent of a modern-day industrial park. The range of businesses included an olive press, a winery, and copper smelting works.[185] An earthquake leveled the buildings centuries ago, but perfume bottles, mixing jugs, and over 60 stills were well preserved. Scientists reconstituted twelve of these early perfumes from the traces of scents found in clay bottles. Extracts of anise, pine, coriander, bergamot, almond, and parsley were among the ingredients.[186]

Perfumes have had many uses through the centuries. Expert Erin Branham documented their value: "They could be holy, used in the worship of the gods or the burial of the dead; they could be a symbol of status and superiority, used by athletes, aristocrats, politicians, and royalty; they could be medicinal, used to relieve ailments of the lungs or skin. In ancient Egypt, Greece, and across the Roman Empire, perfume was part of ritual, beauty, and com-merce—much as it is today."[187]

The most common use of perfume in ancient times was to cover up the smells of the day. Only the wealthy could afford to bathe regularly, while the masses sweated it out. Greek poet Homer believed that good hosts should offer guests baths and aromatic oils so that any gathering was not offensively odorous. Romans made use of perfume for both bathing and the soaking of their clothes.[188] It was sprinkled generously around homes like air freshener. Alexander the Great had his marble floors washed with perfume. His military tunics were drenched in the liquid. Napoleon trav-eled with no less than 100 different perfumes as he battled across Europe.[189] Apparently it was important to smell pleasant while conquering.

For most of history, perfume was incredibly expensive. The cost of raw materials and the production process made it a true luxury. Flowers used included jasmine, lavender, violets, irises, roses, and mimosa.[190] Growing and harvesting took substantial investment. So did the method of extraction where hundreds of pounds of freshly picked blossoms were distilled by solvent. Aromatic plants, fruits, and woods were often used in combination. A single perfume could be made of anywhere from nine to one hundred individual fragrances.[191]

Perfume production changed in the 1860s with the discovery of synthetic compounds. Manufacturers innovated techniques that maximized the efficacy of ingredients, increased yields, created new scents, all while dramatically reducing costs. These efficiencies came at a time when more members of French society desired the finer things and many desired perfume.

What happened next was interesting. The perfume purveyors did not lower their prices and go after a bigger market. These industry leaders recognized that volume would harm the prestige associated with perfume and damage their ideals. It would cease to be a luxury if more could have it at a lower price. According to professor Eugenie Briot, "traditional perfume producers" chose instead to "reaffirm the value of their products and brands."[192]

The perfume establishment soon faced new threats from brash competitors. Department stores began to produce and sell their own lines of perfumes. Ubiquitous perfume bazaars popped up offering discount products. Both types of retailers threatened to disrupt the established and highly profitable market. The new entrants began to play havoc with quality, distribution, and pricing. So the old guard set out to make these interlopers irrelevant.

The traditional providers responded by maintaining higher prices and emphasizing product quality, uniqueness, and exclusivity.

They did this in two ways. They were highly selective in who could retail their perfumes, and they controlled supply to stoke demand and maintain higher prices.

The perfume battle was fought on ideals and perception. According to Eugenie Briot, "The care taken by the manufacturers to promote their products, and the decision to sell the items in richly decorated boutiques, was intended to impress wealthier customers with the symbolic value and desirability of perfumes, in order to justify their higher prices."[193]

Mass-produced perfume was a leap forward in manufacturing. But the industry's marketing decision is a lesson in staying true to the value and conviction of what you offer. The top perfume providers reiterated their story of affluence and quality. That was the essence of their authenticity. They communicated and delivered that in everything they did. Perfume manufacturers subscribed to product, promotion, place, and price—decades before the concept was articulated in marketing courses and corporate boardrooms. In product, they provided only the best. In promotion, the finer things in life were emphasized. In place, distribution was controlled to protect the image. Finally, in price, they strove for a premium. Surrounding all of this was the perception of exclusivity. This air of exclusivity remains the formula of marketing luxury goods to this day.

This was a pivot point in marketing history. The decision to keep perfume synonymous with wealth created a template and framework for the luxury goods industry that survives to this day.

Distribution remains a key strategy for any luxury brand. Bernard Arnault, CEO of luxury goods conglomerate LVMH, has said, "If you control your factories, you control your quality. If you control your distribution, you control your image."[194] In luxury, image has become a tangible asset and represents an authentic expression of a brand. We know, for example, that a Louis Vuitton handbag could be substituted for a reasonably priced alternative. After all, it is a bag. However, the stores that sell them and the perception of the brand allow Louis Vuitton products to be priced beyond the reach of most consumers.

Modern luxury purveyors owe the category's success to decisions made by the Paris perfumers. History would be different had they chosen to mass market. The fascination with luxury remains strong across the globe. People will pay for personal cachet. The enduring lure of luxury testifies to the strength of the original perfume manufacturer's underlying theory: If everyone can afford it, then it ceases to be luxury. Cheaper perfume would cease to be authentic.

JUST WHAT DOES AUTHENTIC MEAN?

Iain Ellwood, Chief Growth Officer at branding agency Group XP, told me that the marketing profession is having trouble with the notion of authenticity. "It is a bit used and abused," said Iain. "I believe it is about the way we behave, not what we say. And I think that's the fundamental attribute that some of the most successful brands have. They behave in a certain way, and they don't spend a lot of time or effort telling people about it. They simply act."

Said Iain, "The ones that achieve authenticity are the companies that have gotten their employees to understand and deliver the company's vision. Their employees' behaviors make them authentic. Consumers are increasingly looking for more meaningful relationships, so the behavior of employees is central to the authenticity of the brand." Iain highlighted some brands he thinks understand the key role employees have in communicating brand authenticity. "If you look at Warby Parker, Starbucks, or Amazon, every single employee is a brand ambassador and knows how the brand and they should behave. Not surprisingly, these brands have achieved great success while spending very little money on traditional marketing or advertising."

Iain tied authenticity to brand experience. "The operating model of the future is about creating extraordinary brand experiences. At the foundation of those experiences is the way employees interact and behave with customers. How does each employee make a customer feel special? When I go to Starbucks, and the employee smiles and gets my name right, when he writes it on the cup, I feel special. I feel like I've got a personalized experience. These brands have built fantastic love, recognition, and awareness through investing in employees and innovative experiences."

Authenticity isn't built on grand strategies that come down from corporate headquarters. More important than proclamations are the meaningful, special, and personal little flourishes that create an authentic bond between brand and consumer. Iain mentioned the practice of writing customer names on Starbucks cups that creates a bond between company and customer. That began at one Starbucks location and was adopted across its vast network. The "Five Dollar Footlong" that has been successful for Subway for years originated with one franchisee. These relationship builders came from the frontlines, not the boardroom.

Iain described how important small gestures can be. "Companies take one little thing and sharpen it. It is that constant energy to improve on lots and lots of small things that add up to the big difference. This type of iterative and innovative culture encourages individual employees to activate their motivation and energy for the firm. If the firm is engaged to deliver small flourishes, then someone on the job in Atlanta can make a big difference to his or her customers. A real and relevant idea can drive the marketing of an entire business. The firms that understand that the small things make a big difference are the ones that have harnessed their employees most effectively."

I had a client in the forestry business when I worked at Price Waterhouse. MacMillan Bloedel, or "MacBlo," as it was affectionately called, was a substantial enterprise that was bought by Weyerhaeuser in 1999 for $2.4 billion. Now, if you are thinking I am about to share a story about the forestry industry, you are wrong. This story is about a waitress.

While visiting one of the company's facilities in Powell River, British Colombia, my consulting team made a local diner our headquarters. For a few days we set up shop in a corner booth to prepare an interim report. We had the same waitress every day. She was about forty years old and never really stood still. No coffee cups got below half full, and when she visited our table for refills she would share a witticism or an observation. She had heard us talking about our project and how we wanted MacBlo to be less reactive, and that meant employees had to be empowered to change processes to please the customer.

As she filled our mugs she pointedly said, "You got to learn to smile before you can run with a tray." I sat there for five minutes blinking and absorbing the lesson. She was telling me not to expect a conservative company to make a big change overnight. We would have to transition MacMillan Bloedel over time. Her line also addressed the fact that if you nail the basics, you are doing well, indeed. On another fly-by I thanked her for being so responsive and attentive. She said she was happy when making others happy, and with a wink was gone to the next table.

Her style, concern for the customer, and joy in her job created a potent cocktail of authenticity. My favorite exchange over those few days was when she anticipated my need for hot coffee.

As she filled my cup, I commented in appreciation, "You read my mind." She looked at me and said, "Well it certainly wasn't *War and Peace* now, was it?" We both laughed. When you think about it, she exhibited at least three of the time-tested principles of marketing: authenticity, emotion, and storytelling.

No one can be fully authentic all the time, but it is a worthy goal. Steve Jobs of Apple talked about the benefits of authenticity: "Your time is limited, so don't waste it living someone else's life. Don't be trapped by dogma—which is living with the results of other people's thinking. Don't let the noise of others' opinions drown out your own inner voice. And most important, have the courage to follow your heart and intuition."[195]

Philosophers and psychologists throughout history have held the idea of authenticity in high esteem. They have examined our outer authenticity, which is how well what we say and do matches what is really going on inside us.

One problem with authenticity is that it is an abstract notion. To be authentic means being faithful to internal rather than external ideas. That is difficult to attain in our lives, or in our brands, or in our marketing.

Kyle Sherwin, Vice President of Media at Sony Music, offered his opinion of authenticity. "As usual, it's a word that is so overused by an industry that loves its soup du jour that it becomes almost meaningless. The original 'idea' of authenticity was essentially a way for corporations to attempt to not sound corporate in their marketing efforts—or at the very least to stay true to their essence. Increasingly in the social age, it has come to mean a way for brands to be conversational, to be colloquial—a means of presenting yourself as a brand in words, in visuals, in advertising, and in customer service—that is more direct and everyday and friendly than perhaps you have been or you think your competition is."[196]

Advertising Age has labeled "authenticity" as the marketing "it" word of the decade.[197] I think authenticity is important, but horribly misunderstood. Authenticity in marketing is not about being "real," unless being "real" means acting consistently, honestly, and in the best interests of everyone you influence. True authenticity can never fully be realized because competing factors and situations modify the ideal. In fact, consumers treat brands with suspicion at the get-go. After all, brands are out to sell something, so instantly, consumers are skeptical.

What consumers cannot abide are marketing activities lacking transparency. When marketers deliberately choose to put out advertising that does not appear to be advertising, or hire influencers to talk up the brand, or use product placement in television and movies, consumers may disengage with those brands. Consumers are now too sophisticated to be snowed. They have been trained to spot disingenuous marketing.

BEING AUTHENTIC BY NOT MARKETING

At the 1893 Chicago world's fair, several brands were introduced to consumers for the first time, including Juicy Fruit, Cracker Jack, and Shredded Wheat. At the fair, a beer named Best Select won the top beer prize. Several years earlier, Johann Gottlieb Friedrich Pabst began adorning each bottle with an actual blue silk ribbon. After the 1893 win, Pabst changed the name to Pabst Blue Ribbon.

The ribbons added cost, but the little flourish helped the brew stand out and justified the expense. Demand kept increasing to the point that more than 1,000,000 feet of ribbon was used every year.[198] Today, the blue ribbon (now printed on the label) remains the key visual element of the brand, acting both as the cornerstone of the brew's advertising and as a symbol of quality and genuineness. Pabst knew that authenticity was more desirable than exaggeration. He let happy customers drive the marketing. He subscribed to Socrates's contention, "Regard your good name as the richest jewel you can possibly be possessed of—for credit is like fire; when once you have kindled it you may easily preserve it, but if you once extinguish it, you will find it an arduous task to rekindle it again. The way to gain a good reputation is to endeavor to be what you desire to appear."[199]

In the early 2000s, Pabst Brewing Company re-embraced the notion of authenticity after a slide in sales. Neal Stewart, a divisional marketing manager at Pabst, heard a rumor from a sales representative in Portland that "alternative people" in the Pacific Northwest had embraced the flagging lager. It was about the only bright spot in the national sales report so he visited Portland hot spots and conversed with these Pabst-loving trendsetters. These consumers shared a very distinct insight: They hated marketing.[200]

The company decided that being understated in its marketing was the way to grow the business. One subset of the "alternative people" who championed Pabst Blue Ribbon was bike messengers. They loved "PBR," as it was affectionately called. One of the brand's first understated acts was to underwrite cycling contests organized for the bike messenger community.[201]

If any other beer brand had sponsored the contest, the event would be awash in banners along with attractive representatives handing out cans and bottles. Pabst added no advertising and sent no one to attend. The messengers responded by drinking more Pabst. The company was as surprised as anyone by the sudden hipster appeal of PBR. Rather than chase their audience with an expensive campaign, Pabst sought subtler ways to keep up the buzz.[202]

The anti-marketing advocates became the beer's marketers. For a brand that was dying, this was more than a coup. Pabst was sold in 2014 to beer entrepreneur Eugene Kashper who stuck with the authenticity that was sparking new interest in the brand. Pabst even sponsors art contests that have involved putting fan creations on cans.[203]

Pabst even recently returned to Milwaukee where it had closed its manufacturing facilities over twenty years ago. Its new microbrewery includes a tasting room. The company intends to use the brewery to experiment with Pabst recipes for discontinued brands such as Old Tankard Ale, Kloster Beer, and other beers made before Prohibition. The old recipes come from Pabst's archives.[204]

In 2002, Pabst advocates were seen as "alternative people." They were soon labeled "hipsters." Now we have "Millennials." This is a group highly concerned with how they are perceived and seen. They are defining and emphasizing what it means for marketing to be authentic. They hold brands accountable. The Cohn & Wolfe 2016 Authenticity Report shows brands are facing an "authenticity deficit," with just twenty-two percent of consumers agreeing that brands and companies are open and honest today.[205]

Authenticity has been applied flexibly in the world of marketing. When actor Ricardo Montalban was the spokesperson for a new car in 1975 he spoke of the Cordoba's "thickly-cushioned luxury seats available even in soft Corinthian leather." Montalban spoke from a script fabricated by the car's advertising agency. The marketing claimed that the leather came from Corinth, Greece. In reality, Chrysler sourced the materials from Newark, New Jersey. There was no such thing as Corinthian leather. The agency invented it to communicate luxury, and Montalban's smooth accent helped sell the lie.[206] I don't think most consumers would accept such deception today.

KEEPING IT REAL

Branding and marketing expert Mark Tungate sees more and more brands that emphasize "craftsmanship as part of their brand." Consumers increasingly value quality and durability, and they want to buy local. Mass-produced goods do not fit into these preferences and thus are seen as inherently less trustworthy.

Mark said, "Technology is so omnipresent in our lives that we're looking for something a bit more tactile. I sometimes call it 'analog snobbery.' It's like the kind of people who will never buy an e-book, who will always buy the real book; who will never download a song, who will always buy a vinyl album. They have rediscovered cameras that take film. This relates to a need for authenticity, sensuality, something you can actually hold. This is quite a powerful component for a brand."

The quest for authenticity can be tough. Starbucks discovered this with recycling. The coffee chain's efforts for sustainability were sincere but ran into headwinds. Starbucks sells four billion disposable cups every year.[207] Its average customer visits the store six times per month, while an incredibly loyal twenty percent visit sixteen or more times.[208] These frequently returning customers want to feel good about the two hundred or more coffee cups they each discard annually.

In 2008, Starbucks announced that by 2015 it would offer recycling at all company-operated branches. Then came the reality. In 2013 the company admitted it wasn't going to meet its recycling goals by 2015, and maybe not ever. This failure was not due to a lack of commitment, but rather "to the fact that just because something can be recycled doesn't mean it can be recycled economically." Starbucks cups are lined with plastic that must be removed before the cups can become new paper.[209]

At the same time, the coffee company set about to serve twenty-five percent of all beverages in reusable tumblers by 2015. By 2011, the company was serving less than two percent of its beverages in such tumblers. So they adjusted the 2015 goal to five percent and offered lower-cost tumblers.[210] In April 2014, the company issued a white surrender flag statement that put the onus back on customers: "Recycling seems like a simple, straightforward initiative but it's actually quite challenging . . . We will continue to explore new ways to reduce our cup waste but ultimately it will be our customers who control whether or not we achieve continued growth in the number of beverages served in reusable cups."[211]

Starting in 2008, Starbucks has offered a way for customers to submit ideas for new coffee concoctions, more food choices, and improved customer service. MyStarbucksIdeas has collected well over 160,000 ideas, and has incorporated some into the company's operations. Until 2017, the website for submitting ideas showed the ideas offered on a variety of subjects, and gave customers the ability to vote on their favorites. Today, customers can still submit ideas, but the details on what happens to them is, sadly, not available.

Google Glass was the result of the company observing that people had their heads buried in their phones all day long. Why not give them a way to keep their heads up? It may have been too far ahead of its time. In 2014, Google CEO Larry Page unveiled Glass and announced a one-day sale that failed to sway consumers and media.

Glass faced a powerful backlash directly related to authenticity. People felt the technology was being pushed upon them rather than meeting a real need. Early adopters were called "glassholes."[212]

Forbes added Glass to its list of history's all-time worst product launches.[213]

Author Fran Hawthorne has a humorous take on what is now expected of companies. She says today's consumers "want an affordable, reliable product manufactured by a company that doesn't pollute, saves energy, treats its workers well, and doesn't hurt animals—oh, and that makes them feel cool when they use it."[214] The humor is accurate, and so is the sentiment. In order to prove authenticity, a company has to do more than it has ever done before.

Marketing must now help fulfill the dreams and desires of consumers in ways that are natural and organic to them. This is the core of brand authenticity. You cannot just claim to be authentic. You have to strive every day to be so in your own unique way.

Most brands will trip themselves up at some point. However, if the intent is honest, then consumers will forgive most missteps and this can lead to an even stronger and more authentic relationship.

Sportswear apparel company Lululemon has suffered from a series of black eyes in recent years. Missteps have included too-sheer yoga pants, quality issues in stitching and pilling, the company founder's comments on women's bodies, and too tongue-in-cheek responses to these issues.

However, it wasn't consumers who bashed the company for its practices. It was investors. The stock price took a pummeling. Lululemon reacted by changing up top leadership and refocusing on the products and how they are merchandized. Core Lululemon loyalists never jumped ship, even as more and more competitors entered the yoga apparel business.

The company has long invested in the extras that go beyond clothing but stay true to the brand. These experiences include free yoga classes and running clubs. Lululemon also compels customers because it stocks very few of each item and updates selections often, meaning shoppers never know what they'll find. This communicates a certain exclusivity that further enhances Lululemon's authentic experience.

When a brand finds that sweet spot where differentiation and relevance overlap, they are in a very strong position. Customers will find them irresistible and if they can maintain authenticity, the combination provides a sustainable advantage that is exceedingly difficult to displace.

CONCLUSION

"The underlying principles of strategy are enduring, regardless of technology or the pace of change."[215]

MICHAEL PORTER, PROFESSOR, HARVARD BUSINESS SCHOOL,
AND CO-FOUNDER OF THE MONITOR GROUP AND FSG

On Black Friday, 2017, I was in Toronto consulting to an advertising agency and a retailer. For professional interest, I visited the city's Yorkdale Mall to witness the action.

Canadian Black Friday is nowhere near as physical as the American shopping holiday. People politely queued to enter the various stores. There was none of the boisterous jostling at some Walmart in the US that is shown on the evening news every year on this day. Since Canada's Thanksgiving is a month earlier than the US holiday, I wondered why the day after US Thanksgiving is a special shopping day in Canada. I found that it began in 2002 when Canadian retailers invited American consumers to Canada to take advantage of exchange rates.

As I sat in the mall, I could see from my vantage point stores, services, and restaurants. People browsed, shopped, ate, and drank.

The seven marketing principles were everywhere:

SOLUTIONS:
At the massage business, they offered a range of "hands-on" services to take away shoppers' aches and pains.

STORIES:

The Hudson Bay Company drew on its rich history so closely entwined with Canada's own to provide compelling context for its uniquely branded goods.

EMOTION:

The florist tugged at heartstrings to entice customers to bring a bouquet home to a loved one.

RELATIONSHIPS:

The bar at the Italian restaurant was lined with individual patrons who were becoming fast friends, thanks to a California wines promotion.

COMMUNITY:

The bookstore segmented books by genre so customers could easily find the reading material that met their interests.

EXPERIENCES:

David's Tea was providing a clinic on the mixing and matching of various teas to create your own personal blend.

AUTHENTICITY:

The Rocky Mountain Chocolate Factory was not only selling sweet treats, it was making them on-site for customers to witness the process and artistry.

These businesses were proving the thesis of this book—that the seven marketing principles that have worked for several centuries are the ones that still work today.

Increasingly, marketing is technology-led and data-driven. Every company I work with is inundated with data. But data is not making them better at marketing. When I spoke with consultant Gary Singer, he made this point. "On the surface," said

Gary, "every single thing about marketing has changed: access to information, data-rich environments, opportunities to observe and react, instantaneous communication, the proliferation of communication vehicles, time and speed to market. But the fundamentals haven't changed at all. You still must understand the needs and wants of your customer and deliver in a way that makes sense to both of you."

The idea of "making sense to both" is critical today. We are overwhelmed by the promise of technology and the data it yields. Many believe that data will make for better marketers and better marketing. But there's a danger of removing what really drives marketing: its human nature. Businesses run the risk of thinking and treating customers as data points and transactions. Marketing exists to help people, *real* people, make consumer decisions.

Marketers need to enhance their knowledge of customer needs, attitudes, and motivations. Knowing the customer helps a company craft messages that are contextually relevant, makes analytics more actionable, and overcomes internal company silos that can be a barrier to delivering a great customer experience.

APPLYING THE PRINCIPLES

In this book, I have deliberately avoided being too prescriptive. I think how-tos and checklists oversimplify the subject and do not recognize that every business is different. The seven principles provide a framework for creating your own marketing messages. You have to do the work and extract what can drive your business.

The seven principles do not work in a linear pattern. All are in play at all times. Mastering how they work together is the challenge, fun, and reward.

Positioning your offer as a solution, telling a compelling story, leveraging the right emotions, forging mutually rewarding relationships, building communities of action, delivering amazing experiences, and doing it all with authenticity—this is the agenda and framework for marketers.

Take the time to look back at marketing's rich history to leverage the successes and to avoid the failures. Marketing is an ongoing experiment where we try, succeed or fail, and then move on. It is a furious plagiarism where we see what works elsewhere and hope that we can make something similar work for our business.

It is a great time to be in marketing. We are not only called on to anticipate the future, we are here to help make it happen.

NOTES

1   Sheryl Garratt, "Jonathan Ive: Inventor of the Decade," *The Guardian*, Nov. 28, 2009. https://www.theguardian.com/music/2009/nov/29/ipod-jonathan-ive-designer

2   Victor Reklaitis, "Nabisco's Adolphus Green Made Cookies Profitable," *Investor's Business Daily*, Dec. 12, 2012. http://www.investors.com/news/management/leaders-and-success/adolphus-green-made-nabisco-cookies-profitable/

3   Artemus Ward, "An Idealist in Business," *Fame*, New York, vol. 26, no. 1 (1917): 63

4   *Advertising Age* Encyclopedia, "N.W. Ayer & Son (N.W. Ayer & Partners): http://adage.com/article/adage-encyclopedia/n-w-ayer-son-n-w-ayer-partners/98334

5   Dale Southerton, ed. *Encyclopedia of Consumer Culture* (Thousand Oaks, CA: SAGE Publications, 2011), 124.

6   Diana Twede, "Uneeda Biscuit: The First Consumer Package?" *Journal of Macromarketing*, Volume 17, Issue 2 (1997): 85.

7   Mondelez International website. http://www.mondelezinternational.com

8   Randal C. Picker, "The Razors and Blades Myth(s)," *The University of Chicago Law Review* 78, no. 225 (2011): 238.

9   Picker, "The Razors and Blades Myth(s)," 239.

10 Picker, "The Razors and Blades Myth(s)," 248.

11 Steve Lohr, "Can Apple Find More Hits Without Its Tastemaker?" *New York Times*, Jan. 18, 2011. http://www.nytimes.com/2011/01/19/technology/companies/19innovate.html?mcubz=1

12 Gadget Guru, "Akio Morita," *Entrepreneur*, October 10,

2008. https://www.entrepreneur.com/article/197676

13   Joe Sharkey, "Reinventing the Suitcase by Adding the Wheel," *New York Times*, Oct. 4, 2010. http://www.nytimes.com/2010/10/05/business/05road.html

14   Ben Zimmer, Cadillac Thrives as a Figure of Speech, *NY Times*, Nov. 5, 2009

15   Liz Hoffman, Greg Bensinger, and Maureen Farrell, "Uber Proposals Value Company at $120 Billion in a Possible IPO," *Wall Street Journal*, October 12, 2018. https://www.wsj.com/articles/uber-proposals-value-company-at-120-billion-in-a-possible-ipo-1539690343

16   Margarita Hakobyan, "The Uberification of Startups," *Tech.co*, Nov. 12, 2015. https://tech.co/the-uberification-of-startups-2015-11

17   Davey Alba, *Wired*, "Uber Just Launched Its Food-Delivery Ubereats App in First US Cities," March 15, 2016. https://www.wired.com/2016/03/ubereats-standalone-app-launches-us/

18   Kenneth Roman, *The King of Madison Avenue: David Ogilvy and the Making of Modern Advertising* (New York: St. Martin's Press, 2009), 123.

19   Richard Dobbs, James Manyika, and Jonathan Woetzel, *No Ordinary Disruption: The Four Global Forces Breaking All the Trends* (New York: PublicAffairs/Perseus, 2015), 107.

20   Dale Carnegie, *How to Win Friends and Influence People* (New York: Simon & Schuster, 1981), 30.

21   Chip Bayers, "The Inner Bezos," *Wired*, March 1, 1999. https://www.wired.com/1999/03/bezos-3/

22   Arnie Kuenn, "Is John Deere the Original Content Marketer?" *MarketingLand.com*, June 25, 2013. http://marketingland.com/is-john-deere-the-original-content-marketer-2-49138

23   Kerry O'Shea Gorgone, "Marketing Megatrends:

Observations from Arianna Huffington at Vocus's Demand Success Conference," *Marketing Profs*, June 20, 2013. http://www.marketingprofs.com/articles/2013/11036/arianna-huffington-marketing-megatrends-vocus-conference

24 Rikke Dam and Teo Siang, "The Power of Stories in Building Empathy," Interaction-Design.org, January 2017. https://www.interaction-design.org/literature/article/the-power-of-stories-in-building-empathy

25 Sarah Everts, "How Advertisers Convinced Americans They Smelled Bad," *Smithsonian.com*, August 2, 2012. http://www.smithsonianmag.com/history/how-advertisers-convinced-americans-they-smelled-bad-12552404/

26 Everts, "How Advertisers Convinced Americans They Smelled Bad"

27 Everts, "How Advertisers Convinced Americans They Smelled Bad"

28 Everts, "How Advertisers Convinced Americans They Smelled Bad"

29 Everts, "How Advertisers Convinced Americans They Smelled Bad"

30 Lauren M.E. Goodlad, ed., Lilya Kaganovsky, ed., Robert A. Rushing, ed., Mad Men, Mad World: Sex, Politics, Style & the 1960s (Duke University Press, 2013), 122.

31 Tom Altstiel and Jean Grow, Advertising Strategy: Creative Tactics for the Outside/In (SAGE Publications, Inc., 2005), 29.

32 Jim Blythe, *100 Great Marketing Ideas* (Marshall Cavendish Corp/Ccb, 2010), 9.

33 Jim Blythe, *100 Great Marketing Ideas* (Marshall Cavendish Corp/Ccb, 2010), 10.

34 Brian Chesky, Airbnb Blog Introduction. https://blog.atairbnb.com/belong-anywhere

35   Carolyn Said, "Airbnb's 'Live There' Ad Campaign Stresses Local Links," *SFGate.com*, April 19, 2016. http://www.sfgate.com/business/article/Airbnb-s-Live-There-ad-campaign-stresses-7258407.php

36   Margalit Fox, "Martin Conroy, 84, Ad Writer Famous for a Mail Campaign, Is Dead," *New York Times*, December 22, 2006. www.nytimes.com/2006/12/22/obituaries/22conroy.html

37   Fox, "Martin Conroy, 84, Ad Writer Famous for a Mail Campaign, Is Dead"

38   Fox, "Martin Conroy, 84, Ad Writer Famous for a Mail Campaign, Is Dead"

39   Jamie Parfitt, *The Multidimensional Agency: How Marketing 3.0 Is Changing the Face of the Advertising Industry* (JP Publications, 2012), 59.

40   Robert McKee, *Story: Style, Structure, Substance, and the Principles of Screenwriting* (New York: HarperCollins, 1997), 27.

41   "In the Future, There Will Be No Markets Left to Emerge," *Foresightinhindsight.com*. http://www.foresightinhindsight.com/article/show/3043#

42   Jennifer Aaker, "Harnessing the Power of Stories," *Stanford University Center for the Advancement of Women's Leadership*. https://womensleadership.stanford.edu/stories

43   Alexia Tsotsis, "Mailbox Cost Dropbox Around $100 Million," *Techcrunch.com*, March 15, 2013. https://techcrunch.com/2013/03/15/mailbox-cost-dropbox-around-100-million

44   "Flashbacks, *Forbes*, March 9, 1998. https://www.forbes.com/forbes/1998/0309/6105253a.html

45   David Ogilvy, *Ogilvy on Advertising* (New York: Vintage Books, 1985), 7.

46   Parker Phillips, "Alka-Seltzer's 'Spicy Meatball' Grows Better

with Age," Ace Metrix Insights blog, August 28, 2014. http://www.acemetrix.com/insights/blog/alka-seltzer-tbt

47   Greg Hernandez and Greg Johnson, "Taco Bell Replaces Chief, Chihuahua as Sales Fall," *Los Angeles Times*, July 19, 2000. http://articles.latimes.com/2000/jul/19/business/fi-55188

48   Weston Gardner, "Why Isn't Humorous Advertising More Effective?" Bettercopy.org, August 20, 2015. https://bettercopy.org/2015/08/20/why-isnt-humorous-advertising-more-effective

49   Emily Spivack, "The Story Behind the Lacoste Crocodile Shirt," *Smithsonian.com*, June 4, 2013. http://www.smithsonianmag.com/arts-culture/the-story-behind-the-lacoste-crocodile-shirt-91276898

50   Spivack, "The Story Behind the Lacoste Crocodile Shirt"

51   Michael Gass, "Leo Burnett Still Wins Ad Agency New Business 40 Years After His Death," Fuel Lines, January 25, 2012. http://www.fuelingnewbusiness.com/2012/01/25/leo-burnett-still-wins-ad-agency-new-business-40-years-after-his-death

52   "Ad Age Advertising Century: Top 10 Slogans," Advertising Age, March 29, 1999. http://adage.com/article/special-report-the-advertising-century/ad-age-advertising-century-top-10-slogans/140156

53   J. Courtney Sullivan, "How Diamonds Became Forever," *New York Times*, May 3, 2013. http://www.nytimes.com/2013/05/05/fashion/weddings/how-americans-learned-to-love-diamonds.html

54   Sullivan, "How Diamonds Became Forever"

55   Jenni Avins, "What the Diamond Industry Is Really Selling," *Quartz*, February 12, 2016. https://qz.com/614214/what-the-diamond-industry-is-really-selling

56   Michelle Graff, "7 Facts from De Beers's 2017 Report on

Diamonds," *National Jeweler*, September 18, 2017. https://www.nationaljeweler.com/diamonds-gems/supply/5834-7-facts-from-de-beers-s-2017-report-on-diamonds

57   Jeff Daniels, "Blame Millennials: Diamond Jewelry Business in a Rough Spot," *cnbc.com*, June 16, 2016. http://www.cnbc.com/2016/06/16/blame-millennials-diamond-jewelry-business-in-a-rough-spot.html

58   Daniels, "Blame Millennials: Diamond Jewelry Business in a Rough Spot"

59   Giles Turner, "Dyson Points to an Autonomous Future as Growth Continues," *Bloomberg*, February 28, 2018. https://www.bloomberg.com/news/articles/2018-03-01/dyson-s-electric-car-dreams-fueled-by-revenue-growth-in-asia

60   Conversations Staff, "5 Things You Never Knew About Santa Claus and Coca-Cola," *Coca-Cola website*, January 1, 2012. http://www.coca-colacompany.com/stories/coke-lore-santa-claus

61   Conversations Staff, "5 Things You Never Knew About Santa Claus and Coca-Cola," *Coca-Cola website*, January 1, 2012. http://www.coca-colacompany.com/stories/coke-lore-santa-claus

62   "130 Years of Coke Taglines," *Advertising Age*, January 20, 2016. http://adage.com/article/news/coke-taglines/302205/

63   E. J. Schultz, "Coke Replaces 'Open Happiness' with 'Taste the Feeling' in Major Strategic Shift," *Advertising Age*, January 19, 2016. http://adage.com/article/cmo-strategy/coke-debuts-taste-feeling-campaign-strategic-shift/302184/

64   Kristin Monllos, "What Branding Experts Think About Coca-Cola's New Product-Centric Campaign," *AdWeek*, January 19, 2016. http://www.adweek.com/brand-marketing/heres-what-branding-experts-think-about-coca-cola-s-new-product-centric-campaign-169082/

65   Arun Devnath, "Coca-Cola's New Campaign

Unites All Brands," The Daily Star, January 27, 2016. http://www.thedailystar.net/business/coca-colas-new-campaign-unites-all-brands-208000

66 Zachary Crockett, "The True Story of 'The Crying Indian,'" *Priceonomics.com*, September 9, 2014. https://priceonomics.com/the-true-story-of-the-crying-indian

67 Donald Norman, *Emotional Design: Why We Love (or Hate) Everyday Things*, (New York: Basic Books, 2004), 7.

68 Norman, *Emotional Design: Why We Love (or Hate) Everyday Things*, 8.

69 Chris Malone, "Why Tylenol Got a Pass and BP Didn't," *Harvard Business Review*, September 15, 2010. https://hbr.org/2010/09/why-tylenol-got-a-pass-and-bp

70 Paul Friederichsen, "Brands Grow with Empathy," *Branding Strategy Insider*, August 11, 2016. https://www.brandingstrategyinsider.com/2016/08/brands-grow-with-empathy.html#.WNwwsmTysnc

71 Nina Bahadur, "Dove 'Real Beauty' Campaign Turns 10: How a Brand Tried to Change the Conversation about Female Beauty," *The Huffington Post*, January 21, 2014. http://www.huffingtonpost.com/2014/01/21/dove-real-beauty-campaign-turns-10_n_4575940.html

72 Bahadur, "Dove 'Real Beauty' Campaign Turns 10: How a Brand Tried to Change the Conversation about Female Beauty"

73 Bahadur, "Dove 'Real Beauty' Campaign Turns 10: How a Brand Tried to Change the Conversation about Female Beauty"

74 Ann Friedman, "Beauty Above All Else: The Problem with Dove's New Viral Ad," *New York*, April 18, 2013. http://nymag.com/thecut/2013/04/beauty-above-all-else-doves-viral-ad-problem.html?mid=huffpost_women-pubexchange_article

75 Susan Chumsky, "Why Dove's 'Choose Beautiful' Campaign Sparked a Backlash," *Fortune*, April 15, 2015. http://fortune.com/2015/04/15/why-doves-choose-beautiful-campaign-sparked-a-backlash

76 E. J. Schultz, "Ragu Explains the Ad Where the Kid Walks In on His Parents," *Advertising Age*, August 15, 2012. http://adage.com/article/news/ragu-explains-ad-kid-walks-parents/236690/

77 E. J. Schultz, "Ragu Explains the Ad Where the Kid Walks in on His Parents," *Advertising Age*, August 15, 2012. http://adage.com/article/news/ragu-explains-ad-kid-walks-parents/236690/

78 Tom de Castella, "What Is It That Really Offends People About Adverts?" *BBC Magazine*, July 31, 2012. http://www.bbc.com/news/magazine-19048807

79 Ananya Saha, "Spike 2013: 'Emotion Leads to Action While Reason Leads to Conclusion," Campaign India, September 17, 2013. http://www.campaignindia.in/article/spikes-2013-emotion-leads-to-action-while-reason-leads-to-conclusion/419476

80 Nick Mirkin, "Inspiring Marketing: An Inspiration Timeline," *Ceros blog*, September 8, 2014. https://www.ceros.com/blog/inspiring-marketing-an-inspiration-timeline/

81 Amy Gallo, "The Value of Keeping the Right Customers," Harvard Business Review, October 29, 2014. https://hbr.org/2014/10/the-value-of-keeping-the-right-customers

82 Jonathan Mitchell, *Staying the Course as a CIO: How to Overcome the Trials and Challenges of IT Leadership* (West Sussex, UK: John Wiley & Sons, 2015), 132.

83 Jessica Michault, "Putting the Accent on Accessories," *The New York Times*, January 10, 2006. http://www.nytimes.com/2006/01/10/style/putting-the-accent-on-accessories.html

84 Hayley Dixon, "When Chocolate Was a Treat: Vintage Ads Recall Heyday of Wafer-Thin Mint as After Eight Celebrates 50th Birthday," *Daily Mail.com*, December 21, 2012. http://www.dailymail.co.uk/news/article-2251486/After-Eight-Mint-chocolate-adorns-Christmas-dinner-table-celebrates-50th-birthday.html

85 Nancy F. Koehn, *Brand New: How Entrepreneurs Earned Consumers' Trust from Wedgwood to Dell*, HBR Press, 2001

86 Susan Himmelweit, Roberto Simonetti, and Andrew Trigg, *Microeconomics: Neoclassical and Institutional Perspectives on Economic Behaviour* (Cengage Learning EMEA, 2001), 64.

87 Nancy F. Koehn, *Brand New: How Entrepreneurs Earned Consumers' Trust from Wedgwood to Dell*, HBR Press, 2001

88 Gregory Wallace, "Barilla Goes from Worst to First on Gay Rights," *CNN Money*, November 19, 2014. http://money.cnn.com/2014/11/19/news/companies/barilla-lgbt/index.html

89 Wallace, "Barilla Goes from Worst to First on Gay Rights"

90 J. Scott Armstrong, *Persuasive Advertising: Evidence-Based Principles* (New York: Palgrave Macmillan, 2010), 168.

91 Seth Godin, *Permission Marketing: Turning Strangers Into Friends And Friends Into Customers* (New York: Simon & Schuster, 1999), 69.

92 Trefis Team, "Ford Transforming into an Auto and Mobility Company with 'Ford Pass': A Futuristic Move?", Forbes, January 12, 2016. https://www.forbes.com/sites/greatspeculations/2016/01/12/ford-transforming-into-an-auto-and-mobility-company-with-ford-pass-a-futuristic-move/#1afb3c524f5e

93 E.J. Schultz, "'FordPass' Seeks to Do for Car Owners 'What iTunes Did for Music Fans'," *Advertising Age*, January 12, 2016. http://creativity-online.com/work/ford-ford-pass/45047

94 E.J. Schultz, "'FordPass' Seeks to Do for Car Owners 'What iTunes Did for Music Fans'," *Advertising Age*, January 12, 2016. http://creativity-online.com/work/ford-ford-pass/45047

95 E.J. Schultz, "Ford App Helps Drivers Find Parking and More as Automaker Seeks Year-Round Consumer Relationship, *Advertising Age*, January 11, 2016. http://adage.com/article/cmo-strategy/ford-digital-app-helps-drivers-find-parking-spots-rides/302104/

96 Nick Jaynes, "Ford's FordPass App Is the Beginning of the End of Car Ownership," *Mashable*, January 11, 2016. https://mashable.com/2016/01/11/ford-fordpass-app/#8Co1zU6YCSqx

97 Jaynes, "Ford's FordPass App Is the Beginning of the End of Car Ownership"

98 Zach Schonbrun, "Beer Ads That Portray Women as Empowered Consumers," *New York Times*, Jan. 31, 2016

99 Schonbrun, "Beer Ads That Portray Women as Empowered Consumers"

100 Schonbrun, "Beer Ads That Portray Women as Empowered Consumers"

101 Shareen Pathak, "Bottoms Up: One Exec's Quest to Turn Down the Bro in Beer Marketing," *Digiday*, September 12, 2016. https://digiday.com/marketing/bottoms-one-execs-quest-turn-bro-beer-marketing/

102 Schonbrun, "Beer Ads That Portray Women as Empowered Consumers"

103 Schonbrun, "Beer Ads That Portray Women as Empowered Consumers"

104 Brian Solis, "Community is much more than belonging to something; it's about doing something together that makes belonging matter," @BrianSolis, Dec. 2, 2014. http://www.briansolis.com/2014/12/

community-much-belonging-something-something-together-makes-belonging-matter/

105 Simon L. Dolan and Kristine Marin Kawamura, *Cross Cultural Competence: A Field Guide for Developing Global Leaders and Managers* (Bingley, UK: Emeral Group Publishing, 2015), 96.

106 Susan Fournier and Lara Lee, "Getting Brand Communities Right," *Harvard Business Review*, April 2009. https://hbr.org/2009/04/getting-brand-communities-right

107 Fournier and Lee, "Getting Brand Communities Right"

108 Mandy De Waal, "Tupperware's Earl Tupper and the Power of Perseverance," Daily Maverick, February 13, 2012. https://www.dailymaverick.co.za/article/2012-02-13-tupperwares-earl-tupper-and-the-power-of-perseverance/#.WcU5d0qGMnd

109 Randy Alfred, "July 28, 1907: Tupperware's First Burp," *Wired*, July 28, 2009. https://www.wired.com/2009/07/dayintech_0728/

110 Alison J. Clarke, *Tupperware: The Promise of Plastic in 1950s America* (Smithsonian Books, 2001), 54.

111 Clarke, *Tupperware: The Promise of Plastic in 1950s America*

112 Maxwell Tielman, "Art in the Everyday: Tupperware—An American Design Classic," *Design Sponge*, March 2013. http://www.designsponge.com/2013/03/art-in-the-everyday-tupperware.html

113 Jeffrey L. Meikle, *American Plastic: A Cultural History* (New Brunswick, NJ: Rutgers University Press, 1995), 122.

114 Bob Kealing, *Life of the Party: The Remarkable Story of How Brownie Wise Built, and Lost, a Tupperware Party Empire* (New York: Crown Archetype, 2016), 37.

115 Bob Kealing, *Tupperware Unsealed: Brownie Wise, Earl Tupper, and the Home Party Pioneers* (Gainesville, FL: University Press of Florida, 2008), 48.

116 "70 Years of Tupperware, *The World of Direct Selling*, February 15, 2016. http://www.worldofdirectselling.com/story-of-tupperware/

117 Jen Doll, "How a Single Mom Created a Plastic Food-Storage Empire," *Mental Floss*, June 6, 2017. http://mentalfloss.com/article/59687/how-single-mom-created-plastic-food-storage-empire

118 Clarke, *Tupperware: The Promise of Plastic in 1950s America*

119 Paul Nunes and Brian Johnson, *Mass Affluence: Seven New Rules of Marketing to Today's Consumer* (Boston: Harvard Business School Press, 2004) 252.

120 Barbara McMahon, "Sandra Bullock and Jennifer Lawrence to Star in Biopics of Groundbreaking Businesswomen," *The Guardian*, March 7, 2015. https://www.theguardian.com/film/2015/mar/07/sandra-bullock-jennifer-lawrence-biopics

121 David W. McMillan and David M. Chavis, "Sense of Community: A Definition and Theory," *Journal of Community Psychology* 14, no. 1 (1986), 6. https://doi.org/10.1002/1520-6629(198601)14:1<6::AID-JCOP2290140103>3.0.CO;2-I

122 http://www.wildedodge.com/jeep-culture-and-the-jeep-wave.htm

123 Will, "The Jeep Wave," *Media & Community*, May 4, 2017. http://courses.suzannechurchill.com/community-s17/2017/05/04/the-jeep-wave/

124 Will, "The Jeep Wave"

125 Uncle Fishbits, "Musing on the History of the Jeep Wave in Honor of Memorial Day," *Uncle Fishbits*, May 28, 2014. http://www.unclefishbits.com/musing-history-jeep-wave-honor-memorial-day/

126 Jeep website. https://www.mopar.com/jeep/en-us/care/jeep-wave/sign-in.html

127 Heather Pringle, "Vox Populi," *Discover*, June 25, 2006.

http://discovermagazine.com/2006/jun/vox-populi/

128 Pringle, "Vox Populi"

129 Pringle, "Vox Populi"

130 Pringle, "Vox Populi"

131 https://www.lego.com/en-us/aboutus/lego-group/mission-and-vision/

132 Stack Exchange, "Bricks" blog. https://bricks.stackexchange.com/questions/653/is-there-a-convention-for-part-and-or-set-numbers

133 Renee Jacques, "11 Awesome Lego Facts That Will Make You Want to Break Out the Bricks Again," *Huffington Post*, February 28, 2014. https://www.huffingtonpost.com/2014/02/28/lego-facts_n_4862088.html

134 Olivia B. Waxman, "The Number of Ways You Can Put Together 6 LEGO Bricks Will Astound You," *Time*, July 31, 2015. http://time.com/3977789/lego-brickumentary-math-professor-combinations/

135 Liam Lacey, "The Lego Movie: A Subversively Flippant Story About Thinking Outside the Blocks," *The Globe and Mail*, February 7, 2014. https://beta.theglobeandmail.com/arts/film/film-reviews/the-lego-movie-a-subversively-flippant-story-about-thinking-outside-the-blocks/article16727918/?ref=http://www.theglobeandmail.com&

136 Keith Oliver, Eduoard Samakh, and Peter Heckmann, "Rebuilding Lego, Brick by Brick," *Strategy + Business*, August 29, 2007. https://www.strategy-business.com/article/07306?gko=99ab7

137 Tiffany Crawford, "Legomaniacs Converge in Richmond for Metro Vancouver's First BrickCan," *Vancouver Sun*, April 24, 2016. http://vancouversun.com/news/local-news/legomaniacs-converge-in-richmond-for-metro-vancouvers-first-brickcan

138 Crawford, "Legomaniacs Converge in Richmond for Metro

Vancouver's First BrickCan"

139 Crawford, "Legomaniacs Converge in Richmond for Metro Vancouver's First BrickCan"

140 "How Lego Became the Second-Biggest Toy Company in the World," *Financial Post*, October 3, 2013. http://business. financialpost.com/news/retail-marketing/how-lego-became-the-second-biggest-toy-company-in-the-world

141 Ross Marowits, "Mattel Buys Mega Brands, Quebec Company Behind Mega Bloks for US$460-Million," *Huffington Post*, February 28, 2014. http://www. huffingtonpost.ca/2014/02/28/mattel-mega-brands-mega-bloks_n_4873095.html

142 "Definition of 'Brand Tribe'," *Economic Times* http://economictimes.indiatimes.com/definition/brand-tribe

143 Bernard Cova, Robert V. Kozinets, and Avi Shankar, *Consumer Tribes* (Oxon, UK: Routledge, 2007), 108.

144 Robert V. Kozinets and Jay M. Handelman, "Adversaries of Consumption: Consumer Movements, Activism, and Ideology," *Journal of Consumer Research* 31, no. 3, December 2004. doi: 10.1086/425104

145 Jay Moye, "Share a Coke 2.0: The Hit Campaign Is Back, and It's Bigger and Better Than Ever," *Coca-Cola Journey*, April 14, 2015. http://www.coca-colacompany.com/stories/share-a-coke-20-the-hit-campaign-is-back-and-its-bigger-and-better-than-ever

146 Nathan Bomey, "Emojis to Grace Pepsi Products in Summer Campaign," *USA Today*, February 16, 2016. https://www.usatoday.com/story/money/2016/02/19/pepsi-emoji-advertising-marketing-campaign/80602336/

147 "Historic Writing," The British Museum website. http://www.britishmuseum.org/explore/themes/writing/historic_writing.aspx

148 Rowan Gibson, ed., *Rethinking the Future: Rethinking*

Business, Principles, Competition, Control & Complexity, Leadership, Markets and the World (London: Nicholas Brealey Publishing, 2011), 218.

149 Nigel Hollis, *Brand Premium: How Smart Brands Make More Money* (New York: Plagrave Macmillan, 2013), 96.

150 "Case Study: AmEx Small Business Saturday," *D&AD*. https://www.dandad.org/en/d-ad-amex-small-business-saturday-case-study-insights/

151 Danilee Diaz, "The Obamas Reveal 2015 Small Business Saturday Book List," *CNN Politics*, November 28, 2015. http://www.cnn.com/2015/11/28/politics/obama-small-business-saturday-reading-list-books/index.html

152 American Express website. https://www.americanexpress.com/us/small-business/shop-small/

153 "Gartner Outlines 10 Consumer Macro Trends to Impact Technology, Media and Service Providers for Next 10 Years," *Gartner*, April 16, 2012. http://www.gartner.com/newsroom/id/1984415

154 John Greathouse, "5 Time-Tested Success Tips from Amazon Founder Jeff Bezos," *Forbes*, April 30, 2013. https://www.forbes.com/sites/johngreathouse/2013/04/30/5-time-tested-success-tips-from-amazon-founder-jeff-bezos/#5812c920370c

155 "Garraway's Coffee House," *London Details* blog, October 6, 2012. https://baldwinhamey.wordpress.com/2012/10/06/garraways-coffee-house/

156 Ben Johnson, "English Coffeehouses, Penny Universities," *Historic UK*. https://www.historic-uk.com/CultureUK/English-Coffeehouses-Penny-Universities/

157 Brian Cowan, *The Social Life of Coffee: The Emergence of the British Coffeehouse* (New Haven: Yale University Press, 2005), 91.

158 Harold C. Whitford, "Expos'd to Sale: the Marketing of

Goods and Services in Seventeenth-Century England as Revealed by Advertisements in Contemporary Newspapers and Periodicals," *Bulletin of the New York Public Library* LXXI (1967).

159 Whitford, "Expos'd to Sale: the Marketing of Goods and Services in Seventeenth-Century England as Revealed by Advertisements in Contemporary Newspapers and Periodicals"

160 Cowan, *The Social Life of Coffee: The Emergence of the British Coffeehouse*, 156.

161 Matthew Green, "The Surprising History of London's Fascinating (but Forgotten) Coffeehouses," *The Telegraph*, March 6, 2017

162 Catherine M. Tucker, *Coffee Culture: Local Experiences, Global Connections* (New York: Routledge, 2011), 7.

163 Amit Kumar, Matthew A. Killingsworth, and Thomas Gilovich, "Waiting for Merlot: Anticipatory Consumption of Experiential and Material Purchases," *Psychological Science* 25, no. 10 (October 2014), https://doi.org/10.1177/0956797614546556.

164 Paul Lukas and Maggie Overfelt, "H. J. Heinz: At a Time When Prepared Food Was a Shady Business, Heinz's Transparent Jars, Factory Tours, and Focus On Food Safety Made His Store-Bought Condiments King," *CNN Money*, April 1, 2003. http://money.cnn.com/magazines/fsb/fsb_archive/2003/04/01/341007/

165 Debbie Foster and Jack Kennedy, *H. J. Heinz Company* (Pennsylvania, Arcadia Publishing, 2006), 44.

166 Quentin R. Skrabec, Jr., *H. J. Heinz: A Biography* (North Carolina: McFarland & Company, 2009), 210.

167 Skrabec, *H. J. Heinz: A Biography*, 134.

168 Robert L. Williams, Jr. and Helena A. Williams, *Vintage Marketing Differentiation: The Origins of Marketing and*

Branding Strategies (Springer, 2017), 57.

169 "Trivia," Heinz website. http://www.heinz.com.hk/en/
Trivia/TomatoKetchup.html

170 "Trivia," Heinz website.

171 Alice Rawsthorn, "An Icon, Despite Itself," *The New
York Times*, April 12, 2009. http://www.nytimes.
com/2009/04/13/fashion/13iht-design13.html?mcubz=1

172 "Heinz Bought by Warren Buffett's Berkshire Hathaway for
$28Bn," *BBC News*, February 14, 2013. http://www.bbc.
com/news/business-21461779

173 "At Last! Heinz Comes Up with the Answer to Opening
Those Fiddly Ketchup Sachets," *Daily Mail*, February 5,
2010. http://www.dailymail.co.uk/news/article-1248814/
Heinz-new-ketchup-packet-How-Dip--Squeeze-answer-
opening-fiddly-ketchup-sachets.html

174 "Heinz Creates New 'Dip and Squeeze'
Ketchup Packet," *New York Post*, September
19, 2011. http://nypost.com/2011/09/19/
heinz-creates-new-dip-and-squeeze-ketchup-packet/

175 Alex Palmer, "How Singer Won the Sewing Machine
War," *Smithsonian*, July 14, 2015. https://www.
smithsonianmag.com/smithsonian-institution/
how-singer-won-sewing-machine-war-180955919/

176 Rosie Baker, "Topshop Partners Google for Interactive
Catwalk," *MarketingWeek*, February 13, 2013.
https://www.marketingweek.com/2013/02/13/
topshop-partners-google-for-interactive-catwalk/

177 Caroline Baldwin, "Topshop Forges Big Data Partnership
with Twitter for London Fashion Week," *Retail Week*,
February 18, 2015. https://www.retail-week.com/sectors/
fashion/topshop-forges-big-data-partnership-with-twitter-
for-london-fashion-week/5072169.article

178 Anjali Mullany, "Customize the Catwalk: Topshop

and Facebook Partner on a Social Runway for London Fashion Week," *Fast Company*, September 13, 2012. https://www.fastcompany.com/1681593/customize-the-catwalk-topshop-and-facebook-partner-on-a-social-runway-for-london-fashion-wee

179 Ironman website for Mont Tremblant event. http://www.ironman.com/triathlon/events/americas/ironkids/mont-tremblant.aspx#axzz4jRrZkPaI

180 Spartan website. https://www.spartan.com/en/race/learn-more/race-types-overview

181 Tough Mudder website. https://toughmudder.co.uk/mudder-nation/blog/look-who-celebrating-wear-your-headband-work-day-0?language=en

182 James H. Gilmore and B. Joseph Pine, *Authenticity: What Consumers Really Want* (Boston: Harvard Business School Press, 2007), 174.

183 Giselle Abramovich, "What Is 'Authenticity' in Marketing?" *Digiday*, February 20, 2013. https://digiday.com/marketing/what-is-authenticity-in-marketing/

184 Geoff Beattie and Louise Fernley, "The Age of Authenticity," Research report, Cohn & Wolfe, November 2014. http://www.cohnwolfe.com/sites/default/files/2014%20Authentic%20Brands%20Executive%20Summary.pdf

185 M. Antoniades Winery website. http://www.antoniadeswinery.com/winehistory.php

186 John Roach, "Oldest Perfumes Found on 'Aphrodite's Island'," *National Geographic*, March 29, 2007. http://news.nationalgeographic.com/news/2007/03/070329-oldest-perfumes.html

187 Erin Branham, "The Scent of Love: Ancient Perfumes," *The Iris* blog, Getty Museum, May 1, 2012. http://blogs.getty.edu/iris/the-scent-of-love-ancient-perfumes

188 Stefanie Fontanez, "Body Odor Through the Ages: A

Brief History of Deodorant," *Mental Floss*, February 21, 2008. http://mentalfloss.com/article/18081/body-odor-through-ages-brief-history-deodorant

189 Katherine Ashenburg, *The Dirt on Clean: An Unsanitized History* (Canada: Vintage Canada, 2008), 111.

190 Lizzie Ostrom, *Perfume: A Century of Scents* (London: Hutchinson, 2015), 37.

191 Various authors, *A Guide to Perfume Production: A Selection of Vintage Articles on the Methods and Ingredients of Perfumery* (Read Books, 2011), 44.

192 Eugenie Briot, "From Industry to Luxury: French Perfume in the Nineteenth Century," *Business History Review* 85 (Summer 2011). doi:10.1017/S0007680511000389

193 Briot, "From Industry to Luxury: French Perfume in the Nineteenth Century"

194 Joshua Levine, "Liberté, Fraternité, but to Hell with Égalité!" *Forbes*, June 2, 1997. https://www.forbes.com/forbes/1997/0602/5911080a.html

195 "'You've Got to Find What You Love,' Jobs Says," Stanford website, June 14, 2005. http://news.stanford.edu/2005/06/14/jobs-061505/

196 Giselle Abramovich, "What Is 'Authenticity' in Marketing?" *Digiday*, February 20, 2013. https://digiday.com/marketing/what-is-authenticity-in-marketing

197 Jill Byron, "Brand Authenticity: Is It for Real?" *AdAge*, March 23, 2016. http://adage.com/article/digitalnext/brand-authenticity-real/303191/

198 Matt Soniak, "How Did Pabst Win Its Blue Ribbon?" *Mental Floss*, April 1, 2013. http://mentalfloss.com/article/49782/how-did-pabst-blue-ribbon-win-its-blue-ribbon

199 Hassun Masum and Mark Tovey, eds., *The Reputation Society: How Online Options Are Reshaping the Offline World*

(Cambridge, Mass., MIT Press, 2012), 25.

200 Rob Walker, "The Marketing of No Marketing," *New York Times*, June 22, 2003. http://www.nytimes.com/2003/06/22/magazine/the-marketing-of-no-marketing.html

201 Walker, "The Marketing of No Marketing"

202 Walker, "The Marketing of No Marketing"

203 Pabst website. http://pabstblueribbon.com/art

204 Tom Daykin, "Pabst to Revive Old Tankard Ale Brand," *Milwaukee-Wisconsin Journal Sentinel*, October 7, 2015. http://archive.jsonline.com/business/pabst-to-revive-old-tankard-ale-brand-b99592289z1-331083991.html/

205 "Only 1 in 5 Consumers Globally Feel that Brands Are Open and Honest. Why Does That Matter?" *Marketing Charts*, April 26, 2016. http://www.marketingcharts.com/industries/automotive-industries-67295

206 Terry O'Reilly, "Words Invented by Marketers," *CBC Radio*, February 11, 2016. http://www.cbc.ca/radio/undertheinfluence/words-invented-by-marketers-1.3443147

207 Adam Minter, "Starbucks Has a 'Venti' Recycling Problem," *Winnipeg Free Press*, April 19, 2014. https://www.winnipegfreepress.com/arts-and-life/food/starbucks-has-a-venti-recycling-problem-255853141.html

208 Meredith Lepore, "15 Facts About Starbucks that Will Blow Your Mind," *Business Insider*, March 25, 2011. http://www.businessinsider.com/15-facts-about-starbucks-that-will-blow-your-mind-2011-3

209 Minter, "Starbucks Has a 'Venti' Recycling Problem"

210 Starbucks website. https://www.starbucks.com/responsibility/global-report/environmental-stewardship/reusable-cups

211 Starbucks website. https://www.starbucks.com/

responsibility/environment/recycling

212 John Naughton, "Google Glass Shows the Merit of Failure," *The Guardian*, July 23, 2017. https://www.theguardian. com/commentisfree/2017/jul/23/the-return-of-google-glass-surprising-merit-in-failure-enterprise-edition

213 Eustacia Huen, "The Museum of Failure Dishes on the Worst Products of All Time," *Forbes*, April 30, 2017.

214 Fran Hawthorne, *Ethical Chic: The Inside Story of the Companies We Think We Love* (Boston: Beacon Press, 2013), 23.

215 Keith H. Hammonds, "Michael Porter's Big Ideas," *Fast Company*, February 28, 2001. https://www.fastcompany. com/42485/michael-porters-big-ideas

www.ingramcontent.com/pod-product-compliance
Lightning Source LLC
Chambersburg PA
CBHW021931190326
41519CB00009B/980